Caucasian Rugs of Yesterday

For my wife, Ann, with love and devotion

Nicolas Fokker

Caucasian Rugs of Yesterday

An illustrated authoritative guide
translated from the Swedish by
Paul Britten Austin

GEORGE ALLEN & UNWIN
London   Boston   Sydney

First published in 1979

  GEORGE ALLEN & UNWIN LTD
  40 Museum Street, London WC1A 1LU

ISBN 0 04 746012 1

© 1979 Rahm & Stenström Interpublishing AB
Taptogatan 4, S-115 28 Stockholm
English translation by Paul Britten Austin
Drawings and map by Arthur Hardie
Printed in Great Britain by
Hazell Watson and Viney Ltd

Contents

Writing about Oriental Rugs

THERE ARE various ways of writing a book about oriental rugs. The simplest is to take the existing literature and use a pair of scissors. You just read seven earlier and preferably unobtainable books, and out of them make an eighth. To do this you must have implicit faith in what these pioneers said and that there is no need to check up on it. All honour to them. But since there were no reliable source materials until the beginning of this century, most of their writings were based on guesswork, and many of their hypotheses have afterwards turned out to be quite wrong. Yet for a historian of art to write a book about rugs without having also had many years of practical experience, it must be conceded, is as hard as for a dealer who *only* has such experience. Without a command of both fields it is indeniably easier to take to the scissors.

When I began to write my *"Oriental Carpets for Today"* I had behind me twenty years in the import trade and not a few trips to the east as a buyer. I had chatted with elderly weavers, the old fellows you meet in the bazaars, repairers, yarn dyers — anyone, in a word, I could hope to get something out of, as long as it had to do with oriental carpets. Since the various districts' rugs are differently knotted, made out of different kinds of wool and have differing depths of pile, different warps and different whipping, I made it a sport to try to identify heaps of "mixed bales" with my eyes shut. My fingertips could recognize between 50 and 60 percent correctly. Yes, I thought I was a real whizz-kid when it came to rugs and carpets!

Only when I sat down at my typewriter did I realize the inadequacy of my knowledge. To write an honest book on the subject, I realized, called for a command of Asia's geography, ethnography, sociology and history, not to mention a fair acquaintance with Islam and classical Persian literature. Likewise several languages, to be able to communicate.

These last, at least, I possessed. I already spoke several languages. As for the geography, I knew it well from practical experience. Tabriz, Hamadan and Meched, I knew, are cities in Iran, towns whose names bathe in a golden historical glow. Tabriz had been the ancient Greek city of Tauris; capital of Armenia in the 4th century, it had been laid in ruins by an earthquake and rebuilt by Harun al Rashid's wife. Hamadan was the biblical Shushan, where Ahasverus, king of the Medes, once ruled, and where Esther, his queen, still reposes with her uncle Mordecais in a superb mausoleum. As for Meshed, or Mashhad — the Sacred Place, as it should really be called it's the capital of Khorasan. Millions of Shiite Muslims come to it on pilgrimage every year, the town is still regarded as the eight Imam's personal property. Its name is also associated with Firdausi, author of the great Shahname epic — the King's Book — and with the astronomer and poet Omar al Khayam; whilst at Shiraz, city of wine and roses, the spirits of the epic poet Saadi, and of Hafiz, poet of love, still burn like two candles no one will ever blow out. Almost all the inscriptions one finds knotted into rugs are quotations from one or other of these mediaeval giants.

What I did have to study was the Koran and the history of Islam. No one, as far as I know, has researched the origin of prayer rugs. Everyone seems to assume they have always existed.

Yet Mahomet the camel-driver did not know them; nor does the Koran anywhere command you to say your prayers kneeling on one. Only in the commentaries on it did I find instructions to kneel on something clean, heavy enough not to be blown away by the wind.

Not until the 7th century A.D. did the Arab invaders of Persia make the acquaintance of rugs. For that fanatical horde of horsemen rugs were practical. They could used them both as saddlecloths and as prayer rugs. And to clean them they only had to shake out the sand. Several centuries later, when Islamic architecture was developing and its superb mosques were being built, a woman got a bright idea: she knotted the mosques' prayer-niche pattern into her lord and master's saddlecloth, thus producing the very first prayer rug. After-

Combined saddle-cloth/prayer rug — the original example of the prayer niche motif — made by the Kashgais, a Turkish nomad tribe which migrated to Southern Persia from the Caucasus. It is reproduced in colour on the back cover.

wards, rugs came to have something sacred about them. In places they were even used to cover graves.

Not that prayer rugs have a monopoly of the faithful's knees. In the mosques you usually find only very large carpets, measuring some 18×12 metres. These are usually a gift from wealthy pilgrims. No matter what their pattern, the smaller are all known — even by experts — as prayer rugs. But this is wrong. True, you may pray on them. But only those which show prayer niches — 'mihrab' — are entitled to that proud name.

Ethnography came into the picture when I met Kashgais, Lures and Afshars down in Shiraz, or Bakhtiars in the bazaars of Isfahan, where they'd come to sell the rugs their womenfolk had knotted during the past year. The Turkmen tribes who live in Iran, Afghanistan and Russia, who make Bochara rugs, so similar yet so very different, were another whole subject in themselves. Likewise the Beluchs of Southeast Iran and Afghanistan.

All these topics fitted into each other like cogs, and it took me three years to familiarize myself with them before I could resume writing. That my book had such a success, was translated into so many languages, and went into so many editions, has given me courage and inspiration to write another, this time about the incredibly interesting — yet in the literature grievously neglected — Caucasians. In this second book I have followed the same principles as in my first. When it comes to colours, I have let the colour plates speak for themselves; and before the book went to press have made perfectly sure every nuance agrees with those in the rugs. Apart from the 17th-century Armenian rugs depicted here, I have included no unique rarities, such as one only finds in museums. The ones shown are the various districts' most typical variants available today in the trade. All were made between 1840 and 1910. Since an oriental rug is very much longer-lived than an elephant, all are in admirable condition; and every detail is fully visible.

Rugs of later date than the beginning of the First World War do not fall within the framework of "Caucasian Rugs of Yesterday." That war, and even more so the Russian revolution, led to overwhelming changes in the Caucasus whose effects were felt by even the most isolated mountain tribes, dwelling at the highest altitudes. In most places rug-making ceased altogether, or else was restricted to the tribes' own needs.

A few decades later the Russians, realizing what a big demand there was for Caucasian rugs, organized their large-scale manufacture. Though these products of state-owned workshops sell well, they have very little in common with the original Caucasian rugs, and mean nothing to collectors. The yarn is not hand-spun. The dyes are not vegetable dyes. And the warp is cotton, instead of the characteristic wool. The pattern is too symmetrical. The rugs lack the originals' improvized irregularities, and therewith also their charm. If you did not know they were made by hand, you would suppose them to be machine made. The peoples of the Caucasus and the conditions they live under have changed enormously. The old way of life has gone for ever; and with it the art of knotting rugs. We must regard the old Caucasian rugs of yesterday as relics; the highly characteristic and now utterly extinct craft — or art — of tribes who have lost their identity and become almost mythical.

The Caucasus

TO APPRECIATE a Caucasian rug properly you must know something about the Caucasus itself. Hemmed in by legendary soaring mountains, it is a facinating region, lying between the Black Sea and the Caspian. It seems as if the Almighty had here flung down all the rocks, cliffs and boulders he still had left over after the Creation. According to findings (1977) by Russian geologists using lead and uranium isotopes, the mountain chain was formed 1,300 million years ago, i.e. a billion years earlier than had previously been supposed.

If the Caucasus really was mankind's cradle, it must have been the scene of the most fabulous progenitation. Even as late as the beginning of the present century, some 350 tribes were living in its innumerable valleys, at altitudes up to 2,000 metres. Apart from such peoples as the Armenians and the Georgians, each with their magnificent culture, only a few of these tribes were known to the outside world. To name only a few of the best known: Gurians, Imerites, Khevsurs, Pshavs, Abkhases, Kabards, Svenetians, Ossetians, Kists, Ingushetes, Lesghians, Tushians, Chechens, Balkars, Dargins, Kurians and Kumiks. Not to have heard of any of these peoples is no shameful gap in your general knowledge. Apart from professional ethnographers it is rare for any outsider ever to have done so.

The Tower of Babel, too, must have stood in the Caucasus. These 350 tribes spoke 180 different languages! Most could be fitted into the various language families. But there were others that linguists failed to classify, or even to learn. How these peoples could even understand one another was a mystery.

Little is known about them. Only the Georgians and Armenians have a written history, going back to the 4th century. All the others were illiterate. What they have to say about their own origins is pure legend. Most insist that they were the country's aboriginal and, of course, its most superior inhabitants. One tribe even goes so far as to claim that God created *them* first; after which he made the earth for their footstool . . .

The Armenian and Georgian family trees do not go back quite so far. They regard themselves as the descendants of Noah's greatgrandchildren, Haik and Khartlos. Which sounds fairly reasonable. It was on Mt. Ararat, after all, the Ark dropped anchor.

What we do know is that, even before the Greeks turned up, there were many peoples in the Caucasus: Assyrians, Babylonians, perhaps Chaldaeans, Achadians, and why not Sumerians?

Pompey's Roman legions raised their tents at the foot of Mt. Kazbek. And since time immemorial Hebrews, so-called "mountain Jews", have been living in the highest valleys. They regard themselves as the remains of the Dan, one of Israel's ten lost tribes. Ethnographers think they are the remains of the Khazars, a tribe who adopted the Jewish faith as their official religion and then, a few centuries later, vanished from history. Medes and Persians sailed across the Caspian Sea 2,500 years ago, settling in Baku and along the sea coast well to the north of Derbent. And still today one or another Daghestan tribe speaks a kind of Medo-Persian.

Such a multiplicity of races and tongues indicates that the great migration westwards happened earlier, and on a larger scale, than historians used to think. Fragments of the Scythians and of Attila's archers remained behind in the Caucasus; as did Mongols, Tartars and Kalmucks from Genghis Khan's yellow horde and Tammerlane's house carls. The sons of the Gobi Desert must have been no less captivated by the Caucasian mountains' grandiose beauty, their pellucid waterstreams and rich grazing grounds than anyone else who has visited this unique part of the globe.

Centuries passed. New peoples arrived. The lawless. The oppressed. Peoples fleeing before the onslaught of conquerors. The Caucasus opened its arms generously to them all. Always there was some inaccessible valley, some plateau or forest, where they could find asylum. They only had to raise their tents to find themselves as much at home as there as all the others.

Up in the mountains there even lived a tall blond blue-eyed folk, who can equally well be descendents of the Crusaders as of the Vikings who founded Kiev and then, perhaps, pushed southwards. Whoever was all these peoples' progenitor, one thing is certain. No other human beings enjoyed such limitless freedom as did these Caucasian tribes. Perfect equality reigned. No chieftain or other authority stood between them and God. Their moral code had but one commandment: Thou shalt respect thy neighbour's dignity. A magnificent article of faith, making all statute books superfluous.

The mountain tribes did not know the use of money. Everything, even life itself, was valued in herds. Vendettas were part and parcel of their social sophistication. Murder was common in all the best families. Anyone who wanted to terminate a feud could buy off himself and his family-members, the price of a murdered man being 80 cows; of a woman 60; and of one's mother-in-law – 5! A mother-in-law went cheap; and in some tribes she wasn't even allowed to enter her son-in-law's house for the first twenty years. But Caucasians, like their rugs, have high life-expectancy. So the old girl had time to pay her daughter plenty of visits, even so.

No one got a wife without paying for her. The price matched the girl's beauty. Caucasian girls — especially Georgians and Mingrelians — were celebrated for it, and many cows were their price. What with women being so costly, their abduction was an accepted, if perilous, proceeding. Any bridgegroom who failed to make good his escape before tying the new family tie would be killed by his bride's relatives. Whereupon the feud began all over again, according to the rules of its bloody game.

But the abduction of women had another function, too. It brought fresh blood into tribes whose extreme isolation might otherwise have led to degeneracy. It also brought new ornaments and colour combinations into their rugs. Hardly surprising, then, if Caucasian patterns show such a wealth of variations and imaginative colours as is found nowhere else in this world!

Islam and the Caucasian Rugs

IT IS REALLY very strange that still, after so many years, no one has protested against art historians and museum curators calling Caucasian rugs 'Islamic art.' Not merely were most exemplars — and among them the most interesting — made by Armenians and Georgians (who are Christians); the "experts'" notions about *all* oriental rugs are wrong from beginning to end! *All oriental rugs and carpets ought really to be called oriental art, irrespective of their makers' religion.* Surely the Pazyryk Carpet, found by Russian archeologists in the 2,500-year-old grave of a Scythian chieftain, is ample proof that knotted rugs existed at least 1100 years before the birth of Mahomet? But that the rugs became so widespread is certainly Islam's doing. At the same time its ban on all figurative art rather stifled than promoted the art of making them.

The Arabs were fanatics. They had no eye to the carpets' value, as works of art. Fearing the newly converted peoples might fall back into idolatry, they either burned or ripped to pieces all rugs that showed figures or symbols they did not understand.

For the same reason the Roman Catholic Church banned all figurative painting, an attitude it had inherited from Jewry. Not until Pope Gregory II lifted this prohibition could biblical events be painted on the walls of churches, to help the illiterate understand the priest's sermons. Gregory called these murals "ars idiotis" – the art of the simple-minded. Not for a moment did he realize he was laying the foundations of the future art of European painting . . .

But in Islam the ban was not lifted until the 16th century. Shah Akhbar, the Moghul emperor, permitted figurative painting on grounds that "Allah would never have given artists their talents had He wished them to slumber unused."

Shah Akhbar's example was followed by Shah Abbas, he who developed the suberb city of Isfahan. Not only did he permit artists to illustrate the King's Book; he even exhorted them to design patterns for the carpets being made in the royal workshops. Here were made the two most valuable hunting carpets known to us. Knotted in silk and precious metal wire, one of them is to be seen in the Royal Palace in Stockholm; the other, formerly owned by the Hapsburgs, is today on view in the Museum of Industry and Commerce, in Vienna.

Except for the innumerable rugs depicting mosques, kings and poets, Islam has made no essential contribution to ornamentation. New elements worth mentioning are: the *mihrab* (prayer niche); the arabesque; the spiral with arabesques; a few medallions; and, lastly, the "five-toothed comb" and the hand with outstretched fingers.

The two last symbolize the five pillars of Islamic faith. They signify: 1) Shahada – "There is no other god but Allah, and Mahomet is His prophet." 2) Salat – the injunction to pray five times a day, turning your face to Mecca. 3) Zakat – the obligation to give 10% of your annual income to charity. 4) The Ramadan fast. 5) Jehad – the Holy War against the infidel.

Tough commandments, particularly the last three!

Fortunately, the ten-percent rule is up to a man's conscience; therefore flexible. If seized with pangs of conscience, you can always make a pilgrimage to Mecca. Having walked reverentially round the Kaaba with true remorse in your heart, you can leave Mecca as sinless as a new-born babe.

Ramadan is a stumbling block to the faithful. It turns their whole existence upside down. In Ramadan they eat – and live – at night. But travellers are excused the fast.

The Jehad must be taken much more seriously. "He who slays an infidel, his name shall be praised; and he who falls in battle for his

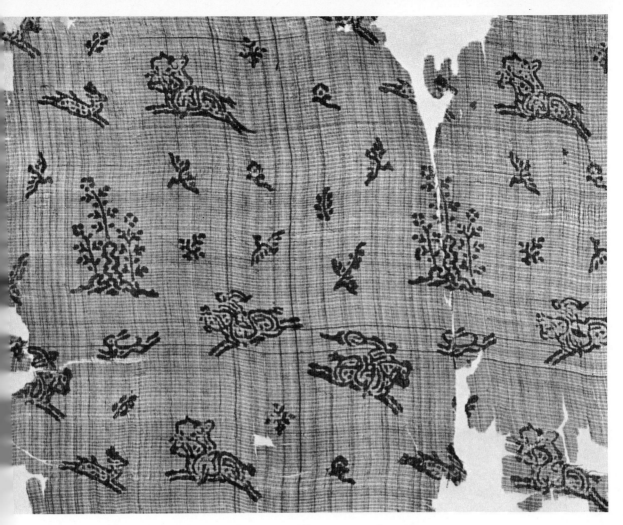

The hunt motif, attributed to Islamic art, really originated in China.
The illustration shows a piece of cloth printed in batik from the
Tang dynasty, 618–906. Not until Shah Abbas' day (early 17th
century) is the hunting motif found in Persia.

faith, verily his bliss shall be great!" saith the Prophet. Muslims believe that if they convert or kill an infidel, or are themselves slain fighting for their faith, they will go straight to Paradise. An attractive programme for bigots, it also explains Islam's unexampled success in converting — within hardly a century — all the peoples from Indonesia to Morocco.

Even today, the faith is advancing in some of Africa's developing countries. Islam is very much a men-only religion. It permits four wives, who can be four unpaid labourers. Paradise, on the other hand has recently lost much of its attraction. Many Muslims drink wine and other alcholic beverages; and houris whose loins smell of jasmine — or Chanel No. 5 — have become fairly common in our modern world. Yet the word "Jehad" is still capable of whipping up latent war-lusts against the infidel.

Caucasia fought its last Holy War in 1830, against the Encroaching Russians. When Kazi Mohammed declared a Jehad with the words "Let the corpses of the infidels be your stairs to Paradise!" all Mongol, Turkish, Nogai, Kirghis, Uzbek, Avar, Chechen, Lesghian, Caucasian and other Moslem tribesmen volunteered to the last man. The mountain roads were barricaded with the corpses of Russian soldiers, and the tribesmen's saddlebags were full of decapitated heads and chopped off hands — tickets of entry to the Muslim paradise.

It took the Russians thirty years to complete their annexation of the Caucasus at the very moment when the West was awakening to the interest of its rugs. Armenian merchants, quick in the uptake, travelled around buying up the nomads' carpets for a song. Since the dawn of time the latter had counted only in cattle. Now they were learning to need roubles; and rather than relinquish their herds, they sold off their rugs for however many they could get. The rugs, after all, had cost them nothing. They had the raw materials close at hand. They sheared their sheep. Sent their children out to gather plants for the dyes. And their women got busy knotting. Since their looms were small, they turned out quite a few rugs each year. The Armenian buyers sold them to buyers from the big European or American firms. Being cheap, Caucasians could compete with their considerably dearer Turkish rivals.

But the low price had one drawback. Private buyers simply did not set the same value on the Caucasians as they did on the very much simpler Turkish ones. Time has set this to rights. Today the Caucasians are valuable rarities, fetching prices far beyond the Turkish; and are infinitely more appreciated for their beauty.

What is Meant by "Antique"?

THE EASTERN peoples' definition of antique is simplicity itself. It's "what you can't get any more."

In the West we see matters differently. Our Customs and Excise accept all objets d'art, silver, furniture, china and oriental rugs as antique and thus free of duty if at least 100 years old. In some countries the Customs have their own experts. In others it is the chambers of commerce and antique dealers' associations which appoint their most highly qualified experts to decide on an object's age and issue a certificate.

People who ask dealers to value their threadbare carpets, destroyed by 40–50 years of ruthlessly careless wear and tear, are deeply disappointed when told their "valuable antique" is a worthless rag, at most only 50 years old.

So how can you see if a rug is antique? Certainly not from its threadbare condition!

Certain features help the expert. Some patterns belong to certain times or epochs, e.g. the Karabaghs' "French roses." Another index of age is the ripeness of the colours. Vegetable dyes, which fade with the passing of time, will look much softer on the face than on the back, which has never exposed to light. A particular brown dye, extracted from walnuts shells and containing ferric acid, eats the wool away almost down to the warp within 60–80 days. A smooth shiny back also tells its tale. The little wool fibres that stick out from hand-woven yarn are not worn away in a moment. Nowadays blowlamps are used to burn them off as soon as the rug is cut down from the loom. This was never done in the old days in the Caucasus. Individual colours, too, tell their tale. Orange, a blend of red and yellow, was unknown until the turn of the century. The Caucasians never mixed their dyes, but used them exactly as they came from the plant. If a lighter tone was desired, they diluted the dye with water, or else did not boil the yarn as long as usual.

And then there's the patina. As well try to describe colours to a blind man! It too tells its tale, albeit a silent one, only to be grasped by the eye and or some sixth or seventh sense. Can you recognize a piece of antique furniture, or wood, or silver, at a glance? Then you'll have an eye for antique rugs. A true expert should be able to fix a rug's age to between some ten and fifteen years. Yet, the Customs' 100 year limit apart, it really doesn't matter a scrap whether a rug is 110 years old or only 99. Unless the year of its manufacture is knotted into it, no man living – not even a clairvoyant – can decide its age to the nearest year!

The few rugs which *are* dated, having their birth certificate as it were knotted into them, are in keen demand among collectors. But they are rare. Few of the rug-makers could read or write.

If you should happen to find a dated rug, you should be able to read numerals and also translate the Arabic date into our own Gregorian one.

This is what the digits look like:

$$\text{١ ٢ ٣ ٤ ٥ ٦ ٧ ٨ ٩ ٠}$$

1	2	3	4	5	6	7	8	9	0

Supposing the date knotted into the rug is 1295. This is how you calculate it:

1) Divide the year by 33 (the 1/33 part which separates the solar year from the lunar year, shorter by 11 days). 1295:33 = 39.
2) Subtract the result from the year. 1295 − 39 = 1256.
3) Add 622, the date in the Christian era at which Muslims began counting from scratch. 1256 + 622 = 1878.

If you aren't too good at maths, there's a key number (583) which will help you to work out the year to within a year or two in your head. Simply add 583 to the date knotted into the rug. 1295 + 583 = 1878.

Try again with the year 1312, knotted into one of the two Daghestan prayer rugs.

1) 1312:33 = 39.   2) 1312 − 39 = 1273.   3) 1273 + 622 = 1895.
The key yields us the same date: 1312 + 583 = 1895.

After the First World War, a number of Karabaghs appeared on the market, dated with *our* Arabic numerals. This took away much of their oriental mystery and reduced the value. On the other hand, there was no need to do mental arithmatic or worry whether they were really antique or not . . .

How to
Identify Rugs

LIKE A much-loved child, Caucasians go by many names. All are inadequate. The innumerable variations in their patterns, colours and borders can make a rug hard to identify. Three different dealers may name three different towns as its place of manufacture, and all perhaps be wrong! They're not doing so badly if they're even right about the district. And with that, unless you're determined to squeeze out some imaginary name, you must be content.

Formerly the Caucasus did not have the hard and fast frontiers it has today. Tribes needed no one's permission to move about. Boundaries, during the thousands of years of Armenian and Georgian history, often expanded and contracted with the fortunes of war. Many people who moved to the conquered districts would remain there even after they had again come under foreign suzereinty. Blood-feuds, raids and persecutions also provided reasons for migration. Hardly surprising, therefore, if rugs showing some particular pattern or knotting style can be found outside the boundaries of their own region.

Both before and after the turn of the century, Western carpet firms' buyers were reluctant to visit the actual places of manufacture. Thus they let slip a chance, while it still existed, of finding out certain facts. The Caucasus lay far from all the great highways. Its terrain was almost inaccessible. Its road network was miserable or non-existent. To penetrate to some of the tribes' mountain abodes would have been as arduous an undertaking for the buyers as joining one of Livingstone's or Sven Hedin's expeditions.

Another obstacle was language. The Greek governor needed a staff of 150 interpreters to communicate with all these peoples. The buyers spoke only English, German or French. So they found it more convenient to set up their headquarters in Constantinople or at Tabriz, and take it easy while awaiting the arrival of the caravans with their carpet bales.

This was a pity. The russification of the Caucasus was still proceeding only slowly. Very little had changed since the Daghestan and Cherkassian Muslims' Holy War had ended with their unconditional surrender in the 1860's. True, the latter had emigrated en masse to Turkey; but that was all. They took with them their patterns; but left behind the "cherkesska," the smartest most masculine costume known since the fig-leaf. Even today, elderly individuals can sometimes be seen wearing the black slim-waisted costume, with its cartridge belt and cartridge clasps over the breast pockets, the Karakul sheepskin cap and the soft leather boots. And of course, the dagger, which no one ever ventured out of doors without sticking into his cartridge belt.

Art historians and carpet pioneers took little interest in the Caucasian rugs. These had reached Europe ages later than the Turkish and Persian rugs, and were regarded as altogether too crude for inclusion in the aristocracy's or plutocracy's collections. An exception was made for the 16th and 17th-century Armenian "dragon rugs", whose origins no one could determine. All the other Caucasians were regarded as degenerate offspring of Turkish prototypes. Which was sheer nonsense. Hadn't the Armenians, the Georgians and innumerable nomad tribes come to the Caucasus more than a millennium before the Ottomans had reached Turkey?

Some later writers merely passed on what the reference books had to say about the height of Mr. Kazbek, Mt. Ararat or Mt. Elbru, devoting only a few brief pages to the rugs themselves. To judge from the wrong names under their illustrations, much of their information had come from ignorant dealers whom they regarded as authorities. But by no means everyone in the rug business is an expert! Gullibility led these authors to specify towns invisible to even the most powerful magnifying glass on any map drawn of the Caucasus in the last 300 years! Or else you'll find them hundreds of miles away from their supposed locations.

Some uncertainty still surrounds the Caucasian rugs. Old Armenian merchants love spinning yarns to respectful listeners. Mostly these are just oriental legends, far from credible as evidence. So — how identify a rug?

Some patterns are so characteristic you can identify them at a glance. Materials and knotting style, too, can be a help. First and foremost, you must realize that the old Caucasian rugs are "all wool". i.e., not only the pile, but also warp and weft-threads must be hand-woven woollen yarn.

The warp can be of undyed light yarn in one district; dark or mixed in another. At a third place goathair may be used for the warp — but only the warp. Goathair is hard, and knife-sharp. Try to knot a pile with it, and you'll cut your fingers to shreds in no time.

The weft-threads, too, are of different colours, light rusty red, blue or white, depending on the district's tradition. The whipping may be single, double, or triple, and its colour too can hint at the khanate where a rug was made. Little technical details, e.g. the way the weft-threads are placed, can make the back look smooth, or, if every second warp-thread is overcast, uneven. Such facts point to one particular area on the map.

One other fact you ought to know: *all Caucasian rugs are made with Turkish — or closed — knots. These are passed around two warp-threads in such a way that what, on the back of the rug, looks like one knots is in fact only half a knot!*

Some armchair expert has called this knot "The Giordes or Turkish knot". Even if the Turks do use the same knot, this name is incorrect. All the rug knotters of the East call it the *closed knot*; whilst what is called as a "Senneh or Persion Knot" is known as an "open knot". All this is better illustrated than described.

Senneh, or Persian — open — knot

But don't let such little technicalities scare you off — you don't have to know how to lay an egg in order to judge an omelette, as Bernard Shaw said. Nor do you need to know how to knot a rug in order to recognise one you find attractive. The interest is enough — plus a little study.

Whilst we know rather a lot, today, about Persian and Turkish knots, a veil of mystery and obscurity still shrouds the Caucasians.

Research has been made still more difficult by the Iron Curtain. Nor have Russian experts got much further, despite having limitless materials at their disposal and no travel restrictions. For them the great problem has been classification. Ought the rugs to be known by place of manufacture, or called after the people who created them? Each is as difficult to trace, today, as the other. And each alternative has its drawbacks. To ethnographers, perhaps, the names of Daghestan sub-tribes are meaningful. But how locate their dwellings geographically? "The third 1570-metre-high valley to the left as you clamber up the mountain's south-east face . . ."?

Ghiordes, or Turkish — closed — knot

The Russians have cut this "Gordian knot" by simply saying a rug belongs in a certain group; e.g. The "Karabagh group" meaning by this that it was made in the Karabagh district, the exact town or village being of no consequence. On the other hand, if a rug is said to "belong in the Kazak group", then it has probably been made in Armenia. Carpets are classified by the Russians exclusively according to the way they are knotted, irrespective of pattern.

This system would simplify my task, certainly. Yet only in emergencies do I propose to follow it. Where I can name the people who made it and, as far as possible, the place where it comes from, I shall. At the same time I intend to rectify some of the commonest errors.

Such names as Kabristan or Kabistan can be dismissed out of hand. No such countries exist, either in the Caucasus nor anywhere else. They are distortions of what ought to be called the Kuba Khanate.

"Kasim Ushag" is probably a spelling mistake, or else has been misunderstood. In both cases no basic research has been done. Nor does the name prove the existence of such a place. What is true is that one branch of the Lesghians — the *Kasimoutchiaks* — made a rug with a highly idiosyncratic pattern. Call it after that tribe, if you like.

Otherwise it falls within the Karabagh group.

Another carpet is sometimes known as "Eagle's Claw" or "Sunburst Kazak", though its pattern resembles neither the one nor the other. What it *does* show is an aura around the Cross — and it is the work of Armenians in the Karabagh district.

"Cloud Kazak" presumably had something to do with the Russian invention of the grouping system. The trade was right in calling it after "Chondoresk", the city in the Karabagh district which is the real origin of this peculiar pattern.

But all these are trifles, compared with the injustice done to all the Greater Georgian, many Azerbaijan and some Armenian carpets, known as "Kazaks".

The very word "Kazak" is easily confused with the Soviet Republic of Kazakhstan, far away on the other side of the Caspian, and having nothing to do with Caucasian carpets of any kind. True, an Armenian town exists called *Kazakh,* where carpets are still being made in State-owned workshops. But neither does it have anything to do with the so-called Kazak carpets. Anyway, the Kh sound in Kazakh is pronounced like the German ch — in *ich* and *doch.*

"Kazak" has more to do with "cossack", pronounced that way in Russian, sometimes also in English. The word is of Tartar origin and means "day hand" or "odd job man". The Cossacks are not a race. Originally Russian or Ukrainian *serfs* who had fled from their feudal landowners, they joined together in huge masses and attacked towns and villages, murdering the men, raping the women, plundering the homes and setting fire to the houses. Cruelty and drink became their chief raison d'etre.

The more famous the Cossacks' exploits became, the more desperados joined them. By the 16th century there were two Cossack republics: the Dnieper and the Don. Anyone who made the sign of the Cross and gave a positive answer to the questions: "Do you believe in Christ?" and "Do you believe in the Trinity?" was free to join. Not that the Cossacks obeyed the Christian commandments, or even understood their implications. Instead, they lived on an undying hatred for Muslims, Jews and Catholic Poles — indeed, anyone not of the Orthodox faith.

Admirable soldiers, they were often used by princes against hostile tribes who threatened their domains. In fact, it was the Cossacks who conquered Siberia from its Mongolian aborigines for the Russians. But in the end the Don Cossacks became altogether too great a power in the state, and Ivan IV attacked and crushed them. A century and a half later the Dnieper Cossack Republic, too, was eliminated.

It was the remains of these hordes who took part in the campaign to conquer the Caucasus. Their efforts were rewarded by gifts of land in the fertile Kuban district, evacuated by the Circassians who had emigrated to Turkey.

The very word Cossack meant the worst horrors of barbarism. Now the Cossacks became the Tsar's feared and deeply hated gendarmerie. And, by a cruel irony of fate, the most beautiful and varied Caucasian rugs from Georgia, Armenia and Azerbajdzjan came to be called after them. An act of injustice as great as calling America after Amerigo Vespuccio.

Ornament

ONE WOULD THINK a country whose neighbours — and, for long periods, oppressors — were Persia and Turkey, must have been influenced by those two great powers' art.

But the Caucasus wasn't. Not the Caucasian people! Certainly, the Persian influence spurred them on to produce better quality rugs: but the Caucasians never adopted Persian patterns. With Turkey it even seems to have been the other way round. It was the Turks who were influenced by the Caucasians.

The flora of their ornamentation indicates that the nomad tribes behind the Urals must have been in touch with Chinese art at least 3,000 years ago. From China they borrowed a wealth of symbols and ornament, using it to embellish their sabres, belts and saddles. Their womenfolk wove it into cloths and flags, embroidered it in their storage bags and tent curtains — and also *knotted* them into their rugs. No printing error: *knotted* them. Anyone who says the Mongols, Tartars and other East Asian nomads were unfamiliar with the art of knotting carpets long before the Age of Migrations is simply being unrealistic. Hadn't the Scythians decorated their tents and their chieftains' graves with high-quality illustrative rugs — 2,500 years ago?

If the Caucasian carpets managed to keep their own character, it was for two strong reasons. First and foremost: *tradition,* more deeply rooted in Asia than anywhere else. And *isolation.*

The Western half of the Caucasus had been Christian since the 4th century. Although many Georgian or Armenian churches were already being built, there is no evidence, either from drawings or engravings, that their floors were ever carpeted. True, Armenians used to kneel in their earliest ceremonies; but each brought his own rug to church with him, and took it home again afterwards.

In the Eastern Caucasus, Islam gained a foothold. Muslims, when they pray, remain seated, kneel, and touch the floor with their foreheads. For them rugs were a practical necessity. Yet no superb mosques of the kind found at Samarkand or Herat, in India, or in Persia, or the rest of the Arab world, were built in the Caucasus. Therefore their women did not have to knot gigantic carpets to cover the floors. All their knotting could be done at small looms. There they went on knotting little rugs, each tribe or family passing down its age-old patterns from one generation to the next.

*A favourite motif, found in the
Chinese flora, and in many
variations in certain Caucasian
rugs, either singly or in rows.
Originally a window or ceiling
design.
Sung Dynasty, 960–1279.*

*Chinese variations (Chou
Dynasty, 1066–405 B.C.) – The
Recumbent S, a motif adopted by
the Caucasians, as also by the
Kurds. The S-s can be used for
borders – horizontally or
vertically – in rows or singly, or
knotted in at random wherever a
blank space had been left.*

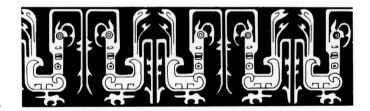

*A cock pattern from the Chou
Dynasty.*

*Patterns from the Ming
Dynasty, 1368–1643.*

Originally each pattern had its own name. These, alas, have been lost. Some of the ones made up by art historians and the trade are as fantastical as any subjective interpretation of an abstract painting. Others seem even ridiculous. "The Kufic Border", seen on certain Shirvan carpets, is a simple piece of Chinese decoration having nothing at all to do with Kufic script. Yet this is the term generally accepted by the trade. "Eagle's Claw" or "Kazak Sunburst" is another instance of uninhibited fantasy.

Another incorrectly interpreted figure is the cock, virtually the trade mark of *Akstafa* rugs. Eighty years ago art historians dubbed it *The Phoenix*. It sounded sophisticated and romantic, certainly. But was a trifle hasty. It is hardly likely the nomads of the Gobi Desert ever have heard the Arabian tale about the bird which flies down to the Nile every 650th year, nests in the temple of the sun god, is burnt to ashes, and comes back to life again. But what nomad doesn't know the cock? For the men he is — and always has been — an admired symbol of their own virility. The Muslims nicknamed him the "Müezzin", his cock-a-doodle-doo being the day's first call to prayer.

The stork, too, has a religious name. Since he spends the winter in and around Mecca, he's known as "Hadji lack-lack" Hadji, of course, being the honorific given to pilgrims to Mecca, and 'lack-lack' the Muslim onomatopöeic for his cry.

The Phoenix, it seems, is a great favourite. One of the world's most famous rugs — to be seen in Berlin — consists of two rectangles containing identical motifs: a bird above a dragon (see colour plate p. 42). Much is said about it in the literature, where the motif is interpreted as "The Phoenix fighting with a Dragon".

Chinese cock pattern, from the Tang Dynasty (618–906), an early variant of the cocks on Akstafa and Shirvan rugs.

Surely this seems more like a bird of prey, capable of attacking a dragon, than a Phoenix? The drawing is of a Tang Dynasty griffon (618–906).

This is plain nonsense. To the Chinese the bird is a peacock or rather, a peahen, and thus a very feminine symbol. But the dragon is a masculine one. So far from fighting each other, they unite in harmony and happiness!

According to an Armenian version, again, the rug was knotted by Armenian hands; and the bird is in fact an eagle – the symbol found in the ancient Armenian kings' coat of arms. And the dragon it is struggling with is Russia, whose Tsars had for centuries been trying to annex the Caucasus. Well, the carpet may be Armenian. That's acceptable. But not the Armenian interpretation of its motif.

Let's look at it logically. If the Chinese had wished to depict a struggle between a bird and a dragon, surely they could have put something fiercer into the field than a peacock? That the Phoenix should have risked his life before building his nest beside the Nile is also unthinkable.

The "Botah" or "Mir-i-botah" motif is found in Chila rugs, and in some from Gendje and Daghestan. The name means "Princely Flower". But the most popular explanation is that it represents a storm-swept cypress. Which, again, is completely wrong. The cypress is a phallic symbol. A bent cypress would therefore have meant impotence; and what man would have dared have cast eyes on such a rug? Or, for the matter of that, what woman? How the motif can ever have got the name "Princely Flower" is therefore a mystery. The immense influence exerted by Chinese ornamentation on Persian and Caucasian rugs only strengthens my hypothesis: that the Mir-i-botah

The Yin Yang Circle is one half of the Chinese Yin-Yang circle, symbol of the union of male and female.

Sevan,
Armenia

An ornament hitherto ignored is the *octagon*. In Persia it is known as "filpa" — an elephant's footprint; in Turkmenistan as "gül" — roses. And in the Caucasus, as far as I know, it has no name at all. As yet no one has aked why the octagon should figure so frequently in rugs from countries thousands of miles apart, as are Afghanistan and Caucasia.

The truth is, the octagon to Muslims and Christians alike is a profoundly religious symbol.

The Georgians' and Armenians' earliest churches were cruciform. But when Rome was still a heathen city their inventive architects had begun building a new octagonal kind.

Additions of the centuries changed these churches' appearance: yet under its conical roof the tower has usually remained octagonal.

Many of these churches and monasteries were built at high mountain altitudes. The site chosen and the octagonal building were equally strategic; they offered a better view — and in more directions — of an enemy's approach. Here we need only mention the St. Hripsimé and St. Gayané churches, the cathedral at Etchmiadzin, as well as the church at Sevan, all in Armenia. And, in Georgia, St. David's Monastery and The Metekhi at Tiflis, and the clock tower at Gelati. Both tell the same tale.

One of Islam's three most sacred shrines the cliff mosque of Quebbel el Sakhra in Jerusalem stands on octagonal foundations. Under its heavily inscribed dome a rectangular grey stone bears the hardly visible imprint of a hand. The Archangel Gabriel clung to this stone, the Muslims say, as the Prophet Mohamet began his ascent to heaven on his white steed El Burak.

The Turkmen tribes' octogons are irregular and cannot be divided up into eight equal segments. They are flat, and usually embellished. You certainly know them under the name "Bochara".

From time immemorial man has expressed his faith, his superstitions, his fear of death, his longing for sunshine, rain, or happy

Plan and cross-section of Quebbel el Sakhara, the cliff mosque in Jerusalem.

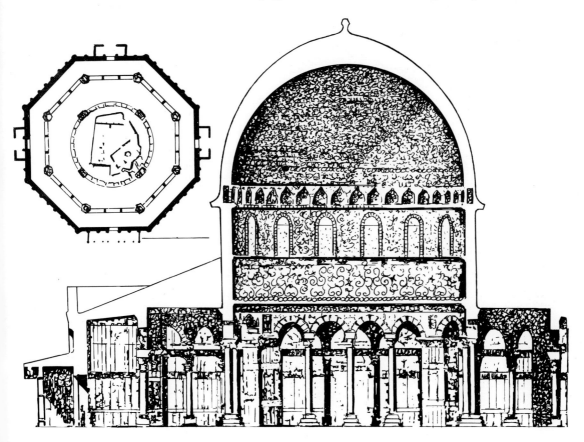

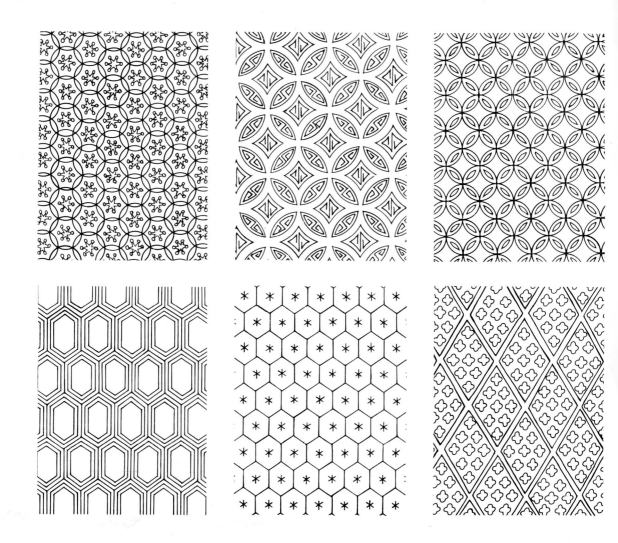

Muslims were forbidden to depict human beings or beasts, so they decorated the tiles of their mosques with geometrical patterns susceptible of endless repetition. Not a few of the original models stem from China. These date from the Sung Dynasty, 960–1279.

hunting, and his anxiety in the face of the numinous powers and enigmas of nature, in magic symbols.

A Baghdad poet wrote that it was only when people found themselves in trouble that they invented God. Since then, he said, God has been their chief trouble. Once invented, God was symbolized by house deities in clay. Certain scripts, e.g. the Chinese, consist of pictograms. One stands for a house. Another for a woman. A female symbol inside a house means 'home'. Two women, inside the same house – 'gossip'.

Religions, political parties, nations, airlines, banks, firms big and small, still like to identify themselves in this way.

Tang Dynasty Flowers (618–906), on which the so-called Shah Abbas design is based: likewise, at a later date, all the so-called palmettes.

Although symbols are found on virtually every rug, their meaning has been forgotten. A Lahore rug-maker whose forefathers had been knotting rugs for innumerable generations told me it was only from my book "Oriental Carpets for Today" he had discovered what he was really doing . . .

To understand *all* the symbols found in Caucasian rugs, you will have to engross yourself in sinology. If the subject interests you or even if you only want to interpret some particular symbol in your rug then I'd suggest you consult some serious standard work. And don't let me discourage you! Take my word for it. Your trouble will be amply repaid in joy and satisfaction at your discoveries. Here are just a few of the commoner patterns, ornaments and symbols derived from various Chinese epochs found in Caucasian rugs.

Buying a Rug

IF YOU REALLY know about rugs you can buy one anywhere. Otherwise you'll do best to turn to a reputable dealer, for you can trust him twice over. First, for his honesty. Second, for his knowledge. Very likely you'll pay him a fairly hefty price; but then you needn't worry whether you've got a good rug, or be afraid it isn't what it's supposed to be. Demand by all means a guarantee, specifying all the details.

If you have your doubts about some rug, ask to have it on approval. But if you're secretly planning to get one of the firm's competitors to value it for you, I must strongly dissuade you. Your chances of an objective valuation are nil. Either the firm will have some much superior rug of their own to offer but much cheaper, or they've just sold a similar one at half the price.

Rather turn to the Chamber of Commerce's or Antique Dealers' Association's official valuer. Pay him his fee. And you'll have a reliable measure of your rug's true value.

Caucasian carpets can also be bought in antique shops. Here you can be less sure a rug really comes from where it's supposed to. But that it is antique you need have no doubts. Indeed antique dealers often have a surer eye for what is really old than many a museum expert. They are less sure of prices and values. Your chances of getting a bargain or paying through the nose are about fifty-fifty.

Caucasians are fairly rare in the smaller carpet shops. But by all means search there too. With a little luck – and knowledge – you may come across your life's bargain. Take a good look around. What's that the proprietor's aged pekingese is sleeping on? A folded Armenian dragon rug, perhaps . . .

Only if you *really* know about rugs, do I advise buying at auction. But take a close look before bidding. Is it worn? Holed? Has it ever been repaired or painted over in places to camouflage wear and tear?

With the back towards you, hold it up to the light. Then you'll immediately see any holes or badly worn patches. The back also tells its tale of repairs invisible from the front.

Minor repairs invisible from the front are of little or no importance. They've been carried out by professionals. Nor are small visible repairs, poorly executed, of any great consequence, providing the rug as a whole is in good shape. You won't have to pay a clever repairer much to mend it again.

Major repairs, e.g. a big hole, such as can only be made good after inserting a new warp to carry the knots, are more serious. Such making good can be expensive.

Equally costly are "cuts" or slashes, i.e. if the rug has been sewn together, instead of replacing the missing warps and wefts and knotting them into the missing part of the pattern.

But worst of all is if one or more small companion strips are missing at one or both ends of the border. This is a common fault, due to the original fringes having been worn away, followed by the narrow weave which prevents the knots slipping off. If a carpet has been looked after as badly as *that,* then the rows of knots will come tumbling off in no time at all. True, it is technically possible to reweave the missing rows along the border; but no carpet repairer west of the Bosphorus is likely to undertake such a time-consuming task. Not to mention the expense!

Otherwise, Caucasians are the easiest of all oriental rugs to repair. Thanks to the elaborate pattern and bright colours, they can be mended quite invisibly – by qualified hands.

For even a 60 or 70 year old rug to have retained its thick pile is rare indeed. *Anyway, a Caucasian with a thick pile isn't as beautiful as one that's had some wear. Wear is an important element in its patina; only then has the pattern achieved its purpose – become a mosaic in wool.*

By "slightly worn" is meant a pile that is at least two or three milimetres thick over the entire surface, thus revealing the pattern down to its tiniest detail. All on one condition: that the rug is densely knotted and its weft-threads properly thrust down, holding the rows of knots in a vice-like grip.

No doubt the trade would dearly like to murder me for saying the pile should be "evenly worn"; rather than "equally short", as the experts say. But neither my sudden death nor my slightly different way of putting the matter can alter the depth of a carpet's pile.

Irregularities in the pattern are not a fault; rather a merit. It's said they are intentional – only Allah can create objects as pefectly symmetrical as a daisy! Actually, no virtuoso is so great that he or she can knot a perfectly symmetrical pattern. Always, no matter how hard it is to discover, there is some asymmetry. Deviations from the pattern in nomad rugs arose spontaneously, to break the monotony of this endless work. But certain apparently meaningless figures may well have been knotted in intentionally. If your favourite rug gets stolen, you can always go to the Khadi, describe it, and get it back.

Another advantage is "Abrash", i.e. one or more horizontal bands of lighter or darker shading, evidence that the rug isn't "made for export". Some collectors are exclusively interested in such rugs; others go in for slightly crooked ones. N.B. only *slightly*!

Lastly, a word of warning. Never bid at auctions for a rug you haven't examined closely at the showing! Held up under spotlights it can look perfectly entrancing. But what tell-tale flaws are hidden in its back? Nor can any catalogue description compare with your own thorough personal investigation.

Yet, when all is said and done, the best advice is — become an expert!

There was a time when for me the Persian rug was *the* Oriental rug. But study of the Caucasians has converted me, captivated me. And I'd wager the loveliest of my prayer rugs against a rusty nail that you, too, will find them more and more fascinating the more you get to know about them!

What Sort of Rug Shall I buy?

A QUESTION altogether too complicated to answer with "it's all a matter of taste". Let me explain.

"What type of Caucasian rug do you prefer?" I put this question to eight respectable dealers and the two leading auctioneers' experts. Personally I've a taste for the Checheni — or chichi rugs, as the trade calls them; and I'd expected at least half my interviewees would share my preference. Not a bit of it! *None* did. Even more surprisingly, all but two disagreed among themselves. And that, I fancy, disqualifies not only my ten experts, but also me, from giving you any definite advice. You must make up your mind for yourself. All I can advise is: have a good look around the carpet shops, borrow a few books on the subject from the library, and try to form your own opinion.

You're thinking of buying a rug to put in front of an antique chest of drawers? Then you'll just have to follow your own taste. And don't substitute anyone else's; because then it'll be *their* taste you're buying, not your own. The dealers will realize instinctively how unsure you are and agree wholeheartedly with your adviser. It's him they're selling a rug to, not you!

But *collecting* rugs is another matter. An expensive hobby, it can hold your whole life in thrall. The only antidote: shortage of cash. Captivated by the rugs' beauty and mystery, you'll relish the little irregularities in their patterns you only discover after months or even years. But when you've got together a real collection, no matter how small, then you've also got a small fortune: a better investment, what's more, than any bank or stockbroker can offer, not to mention the enjoyment you'll have from their beauty and the delights of ownership.

But let's suppose I haven't scared you off rug-collecting. My advice is: *go in for rugs of one and the same kind:* e.g. the Georgian, Armenian and Azerbaijan type known as Kazaks.

There are innumerable variations, both in pattern and colour. In size they measure about 200 × 140 cm., i.e. are admirably suitable for any floor.

An alternative is "Shirvans". Usually the quality is higher, i.e. they have more knots per square foot, the colours are gentler, and they vary in size between 150 × 110 cm. and 320 × 140 cm.

Or if prayer rugs appeal most to you, then buy everything you like and can lay your hands on, irrespective of what district it comes from. Such a collection will soon grow. Each rug measures only about 160×110 cm., though some of the Kazak group are also found in sizes of approx. 200×130 cm.

If you want to make a specialized collection of prayer-rugs, then the "Maresalin" is what you're looking for. Its mir-i-botah pattern can glow with the most fantastic colours. You'll be at a loss to know which to admire most; the rug itself, or the colour sense of the people who knotted it. Maresalis were only manufactured in sizes around 160×120 cm.

Another type of prayer rug – but one so expensive I hesitate to recommend it – is the (in my opinion) overvalued "Daghestan". The central field is almost always light – knotted from undyed yarn – and the whole pattern consists of a grille of rhombs, filled with birds' wings, stylized flowers, or various kinds of purely geometrical figures. At first glance, all Daghestans look alike; but closer scrutiny reveals their variety. The stripes in the borders vary, too. And to find two identical rugs is virtually impossible. The lack of glowing colours is made up for by their quality: and the very best can stand up to the finest Persians. In December, 1977, I saw in a London wholesalers a Daghestan measuring 160×120 cm, such as I could only hold in my hands with reverence. Price to a retailer? Fasten your seat belts, because you've got a shock coming – £4,000, or $8,000! Ten years from now this may seem peanuts. So, let's value it in another kind of currency. Say 10–12 tons of bread! How's that?

But no matter which type of rug you settle for, you must make it the object of exhaustive study. Examine colour reproductions. Read up on it in the literature. And ask every dealer you come across what he knows about such rugs. Ignore the empty talk he'll very likely try to disguise his ignorance with – and you may get the bits missing from your puzzle.

Within no time at all you can become a greater expert on just this particular kind of rug than most dealers. But take care. Don't show off your knowledge or you'll find no more bargains!

If you're toying with the idea of *investing* in old Caucasians, then I'd advise you to buy only the most beautiful and perfect exemplars, even if they cost you more. Between 1967 and 1977, Sotheby's and Christies' prices have risen on an average by 300 percent. And of course the rarities, the very perfect ones, have gone up even more. I've checked with some internationally known dealers, and they agree.

Why am I first mentioning price-rises at auction? The reason is, there are no fixed prices for old Caucasians. As with paintings by old masters, with 18th-century silver, antique furniture or any other antiques, they're worth whatever they'll fetch. All attempts to price them in gold, Swiss francs or any other currency have failed.

Every year, it should be added, an unknown number of Caucasians are lost for lack of proper care and maintenance. The rarer they become, the higher rises their price.

Always there are signs of a further rise; and always there's someone willing — and who can afford — to pay high prices. If you buy a *good* Caucasian, you cannot possibly come unstuck; or anyway not seriously. The Caucasians' increasing rarity will give you a feeling of security. You can get your money back any day you care to, give or take a year. But watch it! A rug has four prices. The one you pay. The sum you insure it for. The price you can get for it. And . . . a fourth price: the one you get when you're forced to sell.

But let's hope yours will pass down in your family for several generations.

Caucasian Rugs in Colour, described

Akstafa

AKSTAFA lies in the north-western part of the Soviet Republic of Azerbaijan. Today the town can boast one of the biggest State-owned rug knotting centres, with a huge output of rugs with neo-Caucasian patterns.

Before the Revolution only a few rugs used to be cut down from Akstafa's looms. Their patterns were commonplace. If you've seen one you've seen the lot. The Akstafa pattern is so characteristic you can't possibly mistake it. The cock, drawn with the naivety of a four-year-old and with one leg outstretched in front of the other. Two vertical rows of such cocks, surrounding three or four polygonal medallions — and that's it.

Other figures — apparently improvized — are the falcon (an immemorial Sumerian fertility symbol) and some four-footed animals which, though originally intended as lions, look like dogs. To the Muslim the dog is an unclean beast he wants neither to touch nor knot into his rug.

The bands along the border are simply a discreet framework for the patterns in the central field, wholly dominated by the cock's broad tail feathers.

To come into its own this rug needs to be of an oblong format. So they are rather long in proportion to their width. The number of knots per square foot is not remarkable, but is compensated for by the knotters' craftmanship. They thrust down the weft-threads so very thoroughly after each line of knots that this carpet, relative to the thickness of its yarn, could be called fairly densely knotted.

The warp is of light grey or light brown yarn. The weft-threads, usually three in number, are light. In view of the yarn's thickness and the three weft-threads, the selvage can only be Persian; i.e., over a single coarser thread.

Some of the cocks were "stolen". We find them in Shirvan carpets (p. 124) and in Soumakh saddlecloths (p. 128).

The Russians place Akstafan rugs in the Gendje group.

Armenian Rugs

FOR PEOPLE with some knowledge of oriental rugs, only the "dragon rugs", found in museums, have anything to do with Armenia. Few know that the "dragon and peacock" carpet, too, is of Armenian origin. Fewer still that the so-called "Marby Rug" to be seen in the Historical Museum, Stockholm, is an Armenian carpet contemporary with these two types.

For a long while art historians puzzled their heads to know how the dragon pattern had reached Armenia, and where it had come from. Russian archaeologists seem to have the answer. New finds, made during their continued excavations of Scythian graves in the Alma Altai district, show that the dragon and other animal figures were parts of the Scythian ornamentation, where it often appeared in pairs, as in coats of arms and . . . in the dragon rugs.

The archaeologists believe these animal figures disappeared from Scythians' ornament when they were converted to Islam. If this hypothesis is correct, it would confirm my conviction: that it's wrong to regard the oriental rug as a form of specifically Islamic art.

A description of the three extant 16th or 17th-century rugs falls outside the framework of this book. Even so, we are proud — for the first time — to be able to show them together.

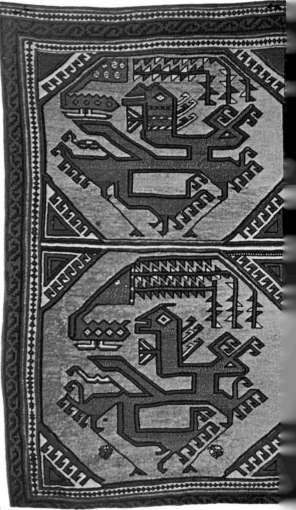

"The Marby Rug," State Historical Museum, Stockholm. Right: "Dragon and Peacock Rug", Kaiser Friedrich Museum, Berlin.

Armenian Rugs

WHAT DO WE really mean, then, by an "Armenian rug?" Is it merely a rug knotted in Armenia? Or should we include rugs made by Armenians outside their own borders?

If the first definition is right, then the Sevan rug would exhaust the topic. Admittedly, other rugs too were being knotted in Armenia up to the First World War, but none so characteristic as to be prototypes. The only exemplar I've ever come across which—as the photo shows—is Armenian in character, is what the trade calls the "Armenian Kazak". This is a rather loosely knotted product, with a mingled brown and light warp, triple light weft-threads and double yellow selvages.

The other rugs, called *Yerevan*, are of "commercial quality" and were made after the First World War. They have no place in this book.

Armenia was already old when Europe was young. Its capital, Yerevan, celebrated its 2750th anniversary in 1967! Within so long a period a country's frontiers can have shrunk and extended themselves over and over again. So have Armenia's. Many Armenians moved into the conquered districts and stayed there even when the fortunes of war went against them, forming little islets of Christianity in the vast ocean of Islam. We find them—and their rugs—dotted all over the Caucasus.

One of the districts completely dominated by them is *Karabagh,* once an important Armenian province. To talk of Armenian rugs is really to talk of Karabaghs. But I've devoted a whole chapter to them.

The Yerevan rug on the opposite page belongs in the Kazak group.

Avar

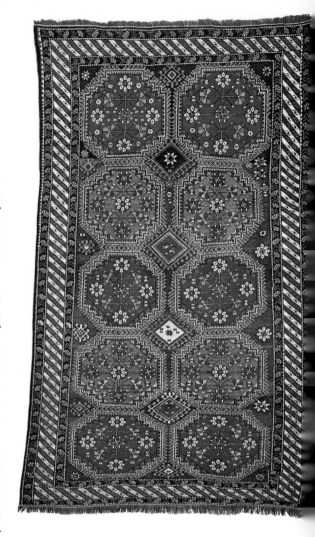

RUGS WITH the highly characteristic pattern here shown were made by the *Avars,* after the Lesghians the largest of the Daghestan tribes. If the name Kuba became attached to these rugs, it was simply because they used to be sold in its bazaars; or perhaps because the town was better known than the tribes.

They are not the same people as the Avars who came galloping with Attila's Huns into the Hungarian puszta, from the steppes of Central Asia. Avaria was a khanate in Daghestan until the early 1830's, when the last Khan and his sons were murdered by the Murids for refusing to join the Jehad against the Russians then being proclaimed by this extreme fanatic movement.

Admittedly, the legendary Avar Hadji Murat, Tolstoy's hero, had his revenge. He stabbed the Murid leader to death in the Ghambzakh mosque. Yet the khanate's fate was sealed, even so. It would have come to an end anyway 25 years later, with the Russian annexation of Daghestan.

Rugs made by the Avars vary in quality from moderate to excellent. The former are soft to the touch; the latter, harder. But the quality of wool and dyes is the same.

Though characteristic, the pattern is by no means original. The polygons in the field are divided up into rectangles in the same fashion as in Moghan rugs; but they are considerably bigger and have no hooks. The oblique strokes are also found elsewhere in Daghestan. But the carnation is the Kuba district's own flower.

The warp is light or mingled with light brown yarn.

The weft-threads are either light or light brown.

The selvages are double and the outermost, at least, are white.

Belongs in the Daghestan group.

Baku-Chila

BAKU IS the capital of Azerbaijan. Among its other overlords have been the Greeks; then the Arabs, Mongols, Tartars, Persians, Turks, then the Persians again; until 1723, when Alexander II of Russia solemnly proclaimed: "We, the Tsar of all the Russias, in whose realms the sun never sets, have decided to take this country under Our gracious protection." Obviously he was more oil-minded than his namesake, Alexander the Great, who had founded Baku exclusively as a place of exile for criminals.

At least 50 languages are spoken in this city. It became a kind of nursery for all the criminals from every land and race in Asia. Crimes not committed here aren't to be found on the statute book. If the daily murder statistic fell below ten, the corpse-bearers wondered what was up. But blackmail was an intellectual profession, since to follow it a man had to know how to write. A short letter to the victim sufficed for cash to be forth coming on the day named. To hand the collector over to the police would have merely made more work for the corpse-bearers.

In a criminal eldorado that offered so many more lucrative occupations, one wonders who could have been interested in knotting rugs? Well, rugs got knotted, even so. The towns of Saliani and Surahani, though they produced no specific patterns that could be regarded as proto-types or points of comparison, were famous. They used dark goathair for the warp and brown weft-threats. The white selvages contrasted sharply against the pattern's otherwise unusually confused tones.

Only at Khila, west of Baku, did the makers persist in always knotting the same pattern, with the same colours. These rugs are easily recognized; above all by the pastel blue, shading to pale turquoise. The pattern is equally characteristic: stepped octagons – or octagons formed as a medallion, surrounded by any number of mir-i-botahs all over the field. Very occasionally a rug may bear the Cross. Others, more especially the Kuba rugs, are strewn with carnations, or

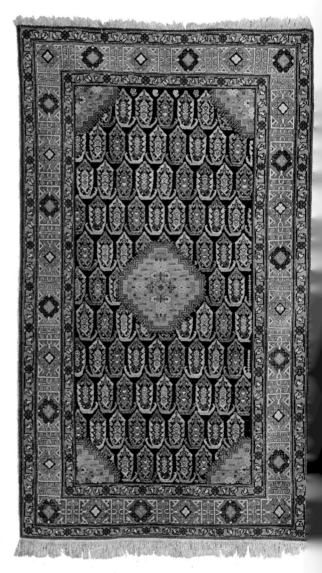

else decorated with the narrow oblique multi-coloured stripes more typical of the Gendje and Daghestan rugs. Individual exemplars with some other pattern are found, presumably the result of inbreeding; but they are rare.

Only the white selvage disturbs the rugs' fine harmony, particularly if they are cotton. The warp can be light, dark brown or mingled. Likewise the weft-threads.

If you come across such a carpet, grab it!

Bidjov

ANY ARTIST who persists in only painting triangles or turkeys will in the end gain recognition as a specialist in his own field. The same applies to Bidjov, a little town in the Shirvan district, where people stubbornly clung to an impossible pattern until they became famous for it.

Perhaps it intrigues you to see how a trained eye looks at a pattern?

The two big sloping S-s are drawn in the same characteristic manner as the Omega — or "cloud" — on Chondoresk carpets.

Above the S-s you can see two stylized birds, facing and *mirroring* each other, exactly like the dragon in the antique Armenian dragon rugs from Kuba.

My section on Armenian rugs mentioned a recent find in the Alma Altai district, proving that the Scythians used to depict pairs of birds and heraldically placed beasts, exactly like the dragons on 17th-century dragon rugs. Or like these two birds.

On the rug's upper section the Crescent is seen in an octagon under a mystical symbol; whilst above them both stands the Cross, on something resembling an altar.

The outer border — which looks more like Chinese waves than the "Running Dog" pattern — is more frequently used in the Kuba district than in Shirvan.

So we are forced to conclude: Chondoresk rugs must have been made by Armenians. And so, it is said, were the antique Kuba rugs. From the Kuba district comes the dominant outer border. The Cross above the Crescent suggests Armenian workmanship. So in all probability the rug is made in the Kuba district by Armenian rug-makers who — or whose families — must earlier have lived at Bidjov.

Why did they stick to this particular pattern? Because it was traditional. Anyway, now that I've analysed the carpet, I don't find its pattern all that impossible, as I did at first. That the falcon looks like a dinosaur, and that the two quadrupeds are supposed to be horses, I even find funny.

Quality: a trifle above average. Ought to feel harder to the touch.

The warp is light, the weft-threads brown and the selvages triple and dark blue.

Belongs in the Daghestan group.

Borchalo

BORCHALO PRAYER rugs from Georgia. The warp is of light yarn. Every other warp-thread on the back is overcast. Weft threads are rusty red. One is introduced straight, two in waves, between the warps. The selvages are quadruple. Two brown and two rust-red. The carpet feels soft to the touch.

Worth noting: How indifferent the Muslims are to the Cross. And . . . what's that there inside the two hexagons? A rudimentary Tree of Life? Otherwise, the Tree of Life is extremely rare as a Caucasian motif. Belongs in the Kazak group.

Checheni

THE CHECHENS are a wild Tatar race, one of the three great tribes who with their many sub-tribes inhabit Daghestan.

Fanatical Muslims, they were the first to volunteer for the anti-Russian Jehad, and the last to capitulate in 1864.

But their hatred for the Russian persists. Eighty years later, when Germany began its drive down to the Caucasus, the Chechens immediately declared for the Nazis. For this, after the war was over, they were deported to Siberia. Not until after Stalin's death were they allowed to go home.

By our standards the Chechens were incredibly cruel. But in chopping off their enemies' heads and hands (the latter only if they wore rings) and in taking them home in their saddlebags as trophies, they were only following the mountain tribes' age-old tradition.

Many Bronze Age artefacts have been found in their country, indicating among other things a primitive phallic cult.

Little more is to be said about their rugs than can be seen in this photo. The pattern is unique. In most exemplars the background is indigo. The other colours, too, are rather sombre. Light shades are rare, and thus more valuable.

Quality varies, too. Some rugs are more closely knotted; others more loosely. But here, too, the rule applies: *age before quality*. In all these rugs the yarn and dyes are equally admirable.

The warp is light or light brown. The double weft-threads and selvages are of light thread.

Belongs in the Daghestan group.

Chelaberd

THESE RUGS are what the trade calls "Eagle's Claw" – or "Sunburst Kazak". They were made at Chelaberd, in the Karabagh khanate, by the Armenian minority.

I have said elsewhere that this pattern is neither a rising sun nor an eagle's claw. Rather, it is a fairly common motif on old Karabaghs. You can see it in plates 105 and 106.

But now – take a closer look at the pattern! The whole of the central medallion is a flaming Cross! Four pistils of the stylized flowers, too, are drawn in the shape of a Cross . . . One only has to realise how deeply Christian the Armenians were, and how chauvinistic, to understand the aura around the Cross, and why it is so cleverly camouflaged that neither their Muslim neighbours nor art historians – nor even authors of books on oriental rugs – have so much as noticed it!

If Chelaberd is one of the most desirable Caucasian rugs, I suspect it's because of its "Eagle's Claw" name. Compare the pattern with the Kasimoutchiaks' (p. 87), and you'll notice points of resemblance between certain ornaments, e.g. the fishbone pattern and the crab-garlands in the border.

The faded red dye, extracted from the madder root, a tint only found in the Karabagh district, is also worth noting. Occasionally, but very rarely, Chelaberds have an indigo ground. Since the indigo came from India, the price for a poor rug-maker was sky-high, and thus he rarely used indigo. Carpets with an indigo groundtone command a price almost double that of the red sort.

Light yarn is generally used for the warp and reddish brown for the weft. Also for the double selvages.

Belongs in the Karabagh group.

Chondoresk

THIS RUG is mostly known under the confusing name of "Cloud Kazak".

Admittedly, a superficial glance might lead you to think this rug, with its big octagons, belongs to the pambaki type of the Kazak group. Closer scrutiny shows certain discrepancies in the technical details. The warp is dark, perhaps even goathair, or goathair mingled with rather light sheep's wool. The weft-threads have the Karabagh district's characteristic pale red colour; whilst the triple selvages are almost black.

Neither does the "cloud" agree. The Chinese never drew clouds in this way. The Chondoresk is a further variant of the distorted Greek Omega, left by Alexander the Great on his way to India. Not that the rug-makers have a clue to what they are up to!

To their credit it can be said they are using the liveliest colours found in any Caucasian rug; and that's saying a lot! The drawback is that there must have been something wrong with the woollen yarn. Perhaps it was spoiled by some inferior dye.

Most such carpets I have come across have been almost threadbare. As for the — not very numerous — exemplars to have survived eighty years of use, they seem to be so much the better for it.

Chondoresk belongs in the Karabagh group.

Daghestan

DAGHESTAN–"Land of Mountains"–is located in the north-eastern corner of the Caucasus. Its valleys have been inhabited since God knows when by Lesghis, Avars, Chechens, Kumiks, Turco-Tatars, Ingushes and dozens of other warrior tribles, always involved in internecine feuds. Strangely, no chronicles were ever written about their women. Though they were the finest rug-knotters in Caucasia, they have remained anonymous like women always have in Islamic countries.

In those regions girls have always been regarded as commodities, to be bought or sold. To marry one you had to pay for her father. Hadn't he supported her all those years? The price was determined by her beauty, graded according to an accepted system: ugly, passable, beautiful and very beautiful. Oddly, it was the "Miss Daghestan" type who was the greatest economic hazard for the father; few young men owned as many cows as he demanded for her. A poor suitor therefore had no other way to get the girl except to kidnap her and take refuge with a friend. In the morning, when he opened the window and fired a few shots in the air, then the whole village knew that the bands of matrimony uniting him to his father-in-law were already tied and the girl had been at least an 18-carat virgin. And all the old man could do about it was to write off his lost capital. If he was lucky, his daughter might would knot him a prayer rug as consolation prize, a handy thing to have around the house in case friends should turn up at the hour of prayer.

That most prayer rugs stem from Muslim Daghestan is not surprising. The colourful species, with superb patterns alive with the tints of the mountain flowers, are generally named after the district or village where they have been knotted – Maresali, Kuba, etc. – and are here described separately.

Prayer rugs made of light, undyed yarn and having the seemingly simplest grill or honeycomb pattern of dark yarn, equally undyed, are simply known as "Daghestani prayer rugs." Experts have always puzzled their heads to know why these densely knotted rugs are so colourless? The explanation is *they were made that way, intentionally, so no fascinating pattern or dazzling colours should distract the faithful at prayer!* These rugs cannot be tied down to any one place of origin. They could have been made anywhere in Daghestan by, or for, fanatically religious people.

Prayer rugs with a similar pattern, often mistaken for Daghestanis, were also made in the Shirvan district. Those are described in greater detail in the relevant chapter.

From that vast mountain area come many rugs whose place of manufacture cannot be determined. Their output had never been significant and their patterns were not what you could call "prototypes." These are known under the collective name: Daghestanis. The multitude of individual designs makes it hard to indicate clearly how to identify them all. However, *all rugs with oblique stripes in their main border are almost 100 per cent certain to have come from Daghestan!*

Warp and the weft threads are of light yarn, likewise the double selvages.

Belongs in the Daghestan group, of course.

Daghestan

Derbent

BEFORE being degraded to the status of an ordinary Caspian sea-port, Derbent was the capital of Daghestan. In Medeo-Persien its name means "road block". From this we can both surmise its function and imagine its visissitudes. Its greatest sight is "Sedd Iskander", a Chinese Wall some 130 km long, erected (according to legend) by Alexander the Great to defend the town against attack from the north.

The town hums with legends of the Macedonian conqueror. The most amusing is that when Alexander died he ordered holes to be drilled in the sides of his coffin, for him to stick his hands out, palms upwards; thus proving he'd left this life empty-handed.

If so, he'd made a big mistake. Surely he could have taken a Derbent carpet? In those days they were certainly better quality than they were at the turn of the present century, when production had become completely commercialized.

Until then Derbent had manufactured lovely fine-quality carpets. The pattern may not have been particularly original – the town was not averse to borrowing its neighbours' ideas; but the colours were so much the more fascinating. No pastel shades; only strong, lively, vivid colours, strongly contrasting with a dark ground that seemed to be a memento of Derbent's violent past. The forceful arabesques, I should add, with their 90° opening and sometimes grotesque animal heads, are the local element in this pattern.

Derbent's 19th-century carpets were of very fine glossy sheep's wool. The warps were light, the weft-threads light or pale blue; whilst for the selvages such yarn was taken as best suited the outermost guard band.

When production became commercialized, cotton began to be mingled with the wool. A bad idea, for wool and cotton take the dye differently and make poor bedfellows. Whoever got this idea dug the grave where Derbent carpets' reputation was eventually buried.

R.I.P.

Gendje

GENDJE WAS the capital of the former khanate of the same name. But don't search for it on the map. When the last Khan fled, fed up with ruling an occupied country, its name was changed to Elisavetpol. Don't look for that, either! Today its name is Kirovabad. At various times the khanate owed allegiance to the Georgians, the Armenians, the Ottomans, the Persians and others. Later, the Russians joined in the game. They captured Gendje from the Persians, who made a surprise attack and took it back again. This dance went on until 1826, when the Russians reconquered Gendje and kept it for good.

Armenians who had moved in during their occupation of the khanate and stayed on when their days of glory were over, dominated its carpet-making. So it was only natural that their carpets, if not in the pattern then in the technique, should have remained deceptively like the ones made in Armenia. This is why some exemplars were regarded as belonging in the Kazak group. Even today Russian experts use the phrase "belonging to Gendje-Kazak group".

In the West, Gendje rugs became enormously popular, particularly the prayer and gallery rugs. The latter were unusually narrow to be "oriental" — about 1 m. broad — and thus served admirably for stairs and narrow corridors. Characteristic of the field were the oblique stripes of various colours, filled with all sorts of motifs except the mir-i-botah, which is only rarely found. The borders, too, were narrow, nicely proportioned to the carpet's width. Border ornament consisted of crabs, stars, running dogs, truncated acanthus leaves, crosses and other nameless Chinese patterns.

The prayer rugs were in demand on account of the peculiar design of their field and the hands in the uppermost corners. These hands end in almost a point at the wrist, as if growing on stalks. A sure identification mark.

The others, with their less idiosyncratic patterns, turn up only rarely in the trade. They are usually family relics. How to identify such a rug?

Ask your grandmother. If she has an infallible memory she may remember where it came from! The warp, however, ought to be of fairly thick yarn, with alternate overcast threads. Nothing is to be deduced from the yarn, as such. Though it may well have been admirable once, it can have become dry as a bone after being repeatedly and disastrously subjected to dry-cleaning which has destroyed the fibres' animal fat. That the pile was long when the carpet was new—especially on rugs with more than two weft-threads—is beside the point.

In the first years of our century production became strongly commercial. Efforts to keep up with the heavy demand lowered the quality. The lower priced rugs were now more loosely knotted, three or four weft-threads to a line instead of the usual two. These rugs were not much to write home about, and soon went out of currency. It was rare for one to survive two generations of owners. But the others, which have survived the wear and tear of the last 60–80 years, may well live to be older than Mehmed Whatshisname, the oldest man in the Caucasus.

Georgian Rugs

GEORGIA is a blank on the rug map. No one, it seems, wants to know about it. Ask an old dealer, and he'll declare he's never so much as heard of a Georgian rug. Yes, though he knows all about Lori, Pambaki, Lambalo, Fachrall, Borchalo and Shulaver rugs, and so ought to be aware that these are all names of towns and districts in Southern Georgia. Nothing of this makes the least difference. Why? Why has the carpet trade always refused to take the word Georgia in its mouth?

The Georgians – or Gruzians, as the Russians call them – are not a homogeneous people. Together with the inhabitants of the three former kingdoms of Mingrelia, Imeritia and Kakhetia, they comprise quite a few other tribes, particularly in the northern mountain regions. Christians, Muslims, and devotees of various home-grown religions, all they have in common is their expertise in knotting delightful rugs whose patterns and colours are without exception both tasteful and imaginative. As one might expect, these rugs are a mirror of this ethnic mosaic! Why, then, are they all known as "Kazak?"

The Georgians are a handsome people famed for their joie de vivre and hospitality. After the First World War the Russians despised them. Georgia, they said, had more princes than it had peasants. Any Georgian owning six sheep, or even a pair of boots, was a prince. And in fact, when Alexander I had annexed Georgia he had guaranteed many landowners with wide domains and many villages their princely titles.

The name of the capital, Tbilisi (Tiflis), means "hot springs". These hot springs were famous even before the Romans called the country Iberia. After a cure at the springs, it is said, even a eunuch can beget children. That Georgia can boast so many centenarians is therefore perhaps not solely due to its yoghurt and garlic.

Whilst the quality from the other countries or khanates can vary fairly widely, the Georgian rugs are all high-class. The sheep from Georgia's high mountains yielded a very fine wool, and the women's hands – trained from early childhood – were extremely capable.

Like the Armenians, the Georgians did what they could to incorporate the Caucasian rug patterns, naively believing that if the carpet ended up in the hands of a Muslim his prayers would be said to the Cross and the Christian God . . .

The picture (right) shows a typical example. The entire carpet is as it were a protest against, or challenge to, the Lesghians, those most fanatical of all the Muslim tribes. Taking their stars and ownership marks for the pattern, the Georgians knotted in a Georgian Cross in lieu of the prayer niche at the top. The Cross was also a decorative element in the light-hued border. The little heart-shaped motifs are from the Chou period (1066–403 B.C.), a curious combination. The carpet was manufactured between 1840 and 1850, the years when the Lesghian Jehad was celebrating its greatest successes against the Russians.

The warp of Georgian rugs is of undyed light woollen yarn; the weft-threads are light brown, varying in number for technical reasons from two to four. In this way, the rugs were prevented from becoming 'wry'.

The selvage is of the same brown woollen yarn as the weft-threads, which may be either double or triple. The fringes, if still present, may be artistically plaited.

Let me add – though it makes my heart bleed to say so – that this rug too, belongs in the Kazak group.

Ingush

THE COLOUR plate shows a rug the pattern of whose central field the Ingush borrowed from their neighbours the Chechens.

Though themselves not Tatars and speaking quite a different language from their neighbours, the Ingush had no less warlike blood in their veins than any other Daghestan tribe.

At the time of the Jehad they were still heathens. Not wanting to be left out of the war, they promptly converted to Islam, and enthusiastically followed the Chechens into battle as enthusiastically as they eighty years later sided with the Nazis against the Russians and after the war — somewhat less enthusiastically — were deported with the Chechens to Siberia.

The rug is a poor imitation of a Chechen. *The difference lies in the border and colour combination; as well as in one crucial detail. Ingush rugs are the only ones in the Caucasus to have only a single weft-thread per line of knots!*

The back looks exactly similar to one from the Hamadan district: the warp is visible at every second line of knots.

Warp and weft are light. The selvage is brown. Belongs in the Daghestan group.

Camel

THIS RUG is not a prototype from any town or district. I include it simply as an example of primitive carpet-making.

Camels are common motifs in both Persian and Caucasian rugs; but always as little figures, spontaneously inserted to fill in a gap between two other ornaments. Here they are large; have two humps; and stand in a long row, like a passing caravan.

Unquestionably this rug was knotted by nomad Muslims, at an epoch when the camel was the swiftest means of transport known to them. Yet the camel was more than a beast of burden. It was also the tastiest — and costliest — of dishes, eaten only on solemn occasions in honour of some singularly honourable guest. Young camel meat tastes delightful if cooked in the fat of the hump and with the right spices.

By the by, there is an explanation why the camel holds his head so arrogantly. Allah has 99 names: the One, the Great, the Powerful, the Merciful, etc. His hundredth name the Archangel Gabriel once whispered into the camel's ear; and it is since that day he bears himself so proudly . . .

The camel is not only extraordinarily patient. He is also very virile. If allowed to mate after an exhausting day's march, the male will do another 60 kilometres without the least complaint.

Concerning the rug itself, there is little to be said; except "age before quality". It is rather loosely knotted and has no outer guard band. But the pattern! Two of its ornaments are worth noting: the "running dog" in the outer border and a Chinese-looking motif in both inner ones.

Belongs in the Kazak group.

Karabagh

IT IS NICE to think that at least some oriental rugs were influenced by western art, not only vice versa.

In Tabriz rugs – to mention only a few such borrowings – you'll find Greek amphoras; on rugs made by the Afghar tribe, oval medallions with female portraits from Michelangelo's Florence; and, on Laver-Kirmans scenes from classical Hellas.

European influence in the Caucasus, is only to be seen in certain types of Karabagh. The impulse came from Russian officers who, fighting to conquer the Caucasus, had been captivated by the beauty and idiosyncrasy of its rugs. But the nomads' rugs were too small for their homes. The Russians wanted something bigger.

The Armenian merchants, who completely dominated the Karabagh rug business, were quick to oblige, set up big looms, organized group work with up to six or eight people working on the same rug, and executed orders for any size whatsoever.

Just then the Russian aristocracy were extremely francophile, furnishing their homes with Louis XV or XVI furniture delivered straight from Paris. So they ordered rugs with the Aubusson patterns they had seen in France, to go with their chairs and tables.

The Aubusson rug was a painted ceiling on the floor, *woven* into a carpet. Its patterns consisted of medallions and garlands of roses. Though the pattern – in Karabagh called "gül franki", French roses – was never the same as in the originals, the district's rug-makers did well out of it for many decades.

These large rugs were also interesting to the western firms' buyers, who saw in them an alternative to the more costly Smyrna rugs. Soon they, too, were busy placing orders. Within a few years the Armenian entrepreneurs had created a major rug-making industry at Karabagh.

To keep up with the demand, the workshops began using extra thick yarn for warp, weft and

Karabagh

pile. This reduced production time by reducing the number of knots per square metre, and magnified the roses. Fortunately, after 20 or 30 years these poor quality rugs wore out. No survivors are now to be found in the trade.

Yet the "French roses" or "Louis Philippe design", as the pattern is called in Europe, went on being manufactured up to the late 1920's. Not that the few rugs to slip across the Russian frontier commanded very high prices, even though their quality — particularly in the smaller sizes — is by no means bad.

Another type of rug which became popular, both in Europe and America, had a smooth dark-blue field with four birds around a medallion. The birds, said the dealers, were parrots, appreciated by Armenians as the only bird able to mimic human speech. This is all hooey from the mysterious East. Probably the bird is a falcon, a fossilized Horus (falcon-headed god of Ancient Egypt) or maybe his coæval, the Sumerian falcon — a fertility symbol — who flew up into a tree, shaking its seed down and fructifying the earth.

But neither were these rugs of any great quality.

Karabagh

Most examplars you still come across are worn down to the warp. Such wear is not due to poor materials; solely to dishonest workmanship.

But along with these inferior, purely commercial products, very high-class rugs were manufactured, too. The rug-makers went on knotting fine old family patterns for their own homes, with thin yarn and many knots to the square inch. Masterpieces of the Armenian rug-maker's art, these are not prototypes, made for export; they are extremely individual rugs, such as the girls were proud to take with them when they married. Such unique Karabaghs command quite hefty prices at auction.

The colours vary from the most exquisite pastel shades to vivid contrasts.

The Cross is a common ornament. As in Georgia, it witnesses to Christian rivalry with the Muslims. Kneeling on such a rug, any Muslim's prayers would ascend to the Christian God. Oddly, the Armenians taught their Muslim workers the pattern, and they went on knotting it spontaneously, without a thought to whether it was Christian or not.

Karabagh is the district that shows the widest range of gradings—from poorest to finest quality. It is here most of the rugs with inscripscriptions—in Armenian of course and datings are found.

The warp and colours of the weft-threads defy definition. They come in shades from the lightest sheep's wool to darkest goathair. But in the very finest rugs the double weft-threads are thin and almost white.

Nor have the selvages any standard colour— unless total absence of white be a standard. In the smaller rugs, no matter what their colour, the selvages are usually double; on the larger ones single, as in Persian carpets.

They gave their name to the Karabagh group.

Karachop

FANTASTIC! That a single rug pattern can put such an insignificant little village as *Karachop* on the map! Administratively it lies inside the Borchalo district of Georgia; but technically and artistically it falls within the Kazak group.

The pattern is as characteristic as a thumb print: four rectangles around a large octagonal medallion. The rectangles are star-spangled, in magnificent colours, the medallion being light and decorated with various geometrical ornaments. The rest of the field is crowded with rectangles and rhombs set with latch-hooks, as well as idiosyncratic C's, welded together, one being reversed, as in a monogram. The most remarkable thing about it is that, despite the overpatterning, the rug does not seem "muddled" or in any way disharmonious.

The border, with its broad central band and its two very narrow comparisons, frames to perfection the generously decorated field.

This was not the only pattern knotted in this village. But the others are neither interesting nor so valuable as the *real* Karachop, as I have described it.

Prayer niche rugs, too, were made; though never, as far as I know, in small sizes. Fortunately, one may add. For with the Karachop rugs' typically high pile they would not have looked well.

Another characteristic is the size, around 225 × 150 cm, a considerably larger format than is usual in other rugs of the Kazak group.

The warp is powerful, usually of undyed grey woollen yarn, of all shades.

Weft-threads are rusty brown and triple: hence the high pile.

The selvage is single-threaded, as in Persian rugs.

Prices at major auctions can vary widely between any two exemplars on the whole equally valuable in respect to pattern, size and condition. A more attractive colour scheme can double the price.

Karagashli

HERE IS a collector's item for the connoisseur who has plenty of money in the bank.

Look at the three rugs depicted. Note the wonderful colours — how the contrast between indigo and madder red is transformed into harmony — the generous space between the four rectangular or *almost* rectangular medallions and the rest of the ornaments. Note, too, the mystical animals; and how it was more than Armenian fingers could do not to knot the Cross into the pattern, however awkwardly they placed it.

When, furthermore, I tell you that these rugs are extremely densely knotted, then you'll understand why they are meat and drink to the collector.

They were made between Kuba and Derbent.

The warp is light, the weft-threads thin och light; the selvage dark.

Belongs in the Daghestan group.

Kasimoutchiak

IN MY CHAPTER on identifying rugs I pointed out that these are wrongly known as Kasim Ushagh or Kasim Ushak, either a misunderstanding of their name, or else some confused association with the Turkish Ushak rugs. They were made by Lesghian sub-tribes, Kasimoutchiaks living in the Karabagh district.

Two remarkable facts should be mentioned. One is that the Kasimotchiaks refused to use any other pattern than the single one traditional in their own tribe. Even women who marry into it from some other are obliged to learn this pattern and forget everything they have done before. The other is, that they only make rugs of about 210 × 140 cm, no larger or smaller.

The absence of small rugs is understandable. To have its proper effect, the yarn would have to be very thin; and this would not be economical. To knot a small rug would have taken longer than to knot a big one. But – did they or did they not make prayer rugs? Presumably they did. But being fanatical Muslims, they must have regarded them as sacred; and thus refused to sell them, lest some infidel tread on them. However this may be, neither I nor any expert I have consulted has ever seen a small examplar, with or without prayer niche.

Whether you like the pattern or not is a matter of taste. Yet it is, one must admit, amazingly symmetrical to have been made simultaneously by two gossiping women who did not even have a blue print to go after. Only a few tiny details distinguish its two halves.

The tribe is small, making up only 6% of the Lesghians. Therefore its output was smaller than the big tribes'. Its rugs are thus collectors' items.

Materials and workmanship are both high-class. The warp is light, the weft-threads a faded reddish-brown, the selvage either of the same colour as the weft-threads or also light brown.

The rugs belong in the Karabagh group.

Konangulkent
or Konagkent

WHILST MANY rugs whose patterns are aesthetically very attractive remain nameless, or else are known only collectively by the name of their district, some other rug with an indifferent design can have brought world fame to the village it came from. As with Konangulkent and its carpets.

Only one map of Caucasia of the last 300 years — published by Verlag des Evangelischen Missions Seminari in Basel, 1825 — shows where it lies. *Konangulkent* is in my view a more correct spelling than the careless Konagkent. It lies ten versts south-east of Seichour. All other cartographers ignored the place, as did the historians, ethnographers and travellers who found nothing there worthy of note. Its fame is thus certainly due to an oriental rug with a labyrinthine and definitely unattractive pattern.

As with most east and south-east Caucasian rugs, the Armenian hallmark is recognizable at a glance. See the five crosses lost amid the confusion of lines! Turn the rug upside down, and you'll see three rows of primitively stylized birds, placed mirrorwise. These are relics of the Scythian ornamental fauna already mentioned in connection with the Armenian and Bidjov rugs.

The only unusual feature of the field is the spruce trees in the hexagons, whose like is only to be found in the Bakhtiari rugs of Persia.

But these spruces must not be confounded with the Tree of Life, a symbol never found in Caucasians. Only once have I ever seen one bearing such a design. A verdant tree does not mean to the fertile Caucasus what it does in the parched lands of the Bible or in Persia, where it symbolized the *élan vital* — the life force.

Otherwise, this Konangulkent rug shows the usual broad and very dominant central band, with its nameless Chinese ornament. The trade calls it, not very intelligently, the "Kufic Border". I'd prefer to call it the "bracket" or "bookends" pattern.

Qualitywise this rug is as good as all the others from the Kuba district, medium quality being the lowest in the scale.

The warp is of light yarn, the weft-threads dark, and the double selvages dark blue.

But this is only half the story.

Konangulkent

There exists another rug *ascribed* to Konangulkent; the one seen on the right. Its pattern is hardly more attractive than the "labyrinth". It too is of some significance in the history of art. It too bears the Armenian hallmark: the central Cross and the four smaller ones in the medallion. But this pattern's really interesting feature is that its cruciform medallion *is the ground plan of the St. Hripsimé Church, one of the Armenians' holiest, and one of their 7th-century architectural masterpieces*!

In comparing the church's ground plan and the carpets' medallion one must bear in mind that the Caucasian carpet-makers were ignorant of the curvilinear pattern. Everything circular on the plan has been transferred rectangularly to the carpet. Nor need we cudgel our brains to figure out how this church's plan should still be found, 1300 years later, in a rug made in a remote country town. That really *is* one of the mysteries of the Orient . . .

But to show his devotion to Christianity the designer drew a line through all the S-s in the border, thus transforming them into D-s. D,

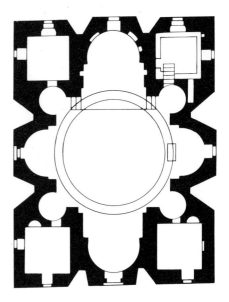

which stands for Dios = God.

When it comes to such a rug, the colour of warp, weft or selvage is of no consequence whatever.

Belongs in the Daghestan group.

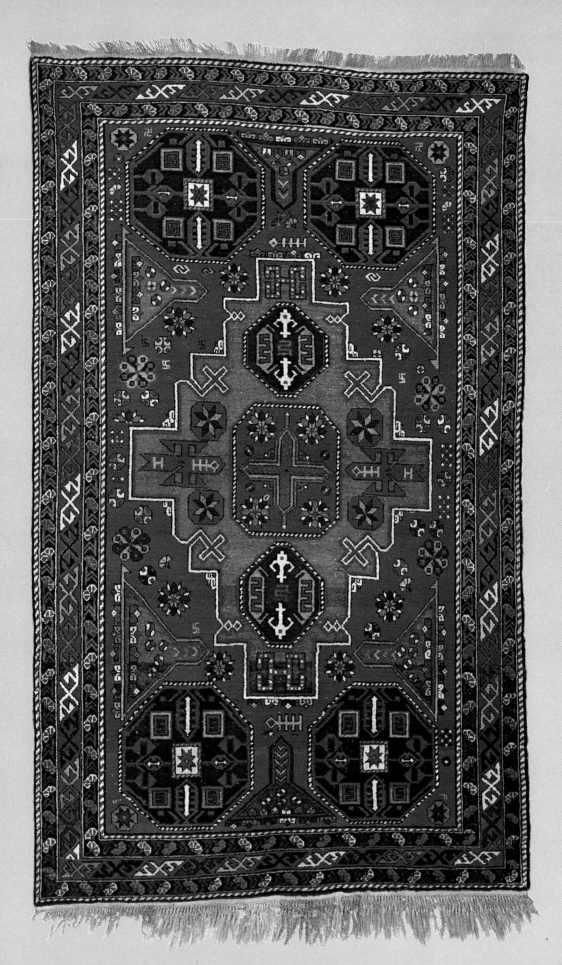

Kuba

THE KUBA BAZAAR was always the centre for its district's rugs. Of the many towns' and villages' products sold there only a few acquired a name of their own – Perepedil, Konagkend, Karagashlis and, above all, Seichour. All the others were known indescriminately as "Kuba rugs".

And if a European dealer's representative asked where some particular rug came from, the Armenian buyer answered with a shrug and a "from Kubastan"; a word meaning literally "the Kuba country", though what he meant was from the countryside – viz. the villages – *around* Kuba. Whence the distortions "Kabistan" and "Kabristan", still widely in use today.

Apart from the Chechens and the above-mentioned towns' highly characteristic patterns, there was only one whose peer was found nowhere except in Kuba. The one to the right. Today we can no longer know exactly where it was made. But the light variant of the *running dog* border, the unique decoration around the rhomboid medallions, and the little ornaments scattered across its field, all these are sure signs of its having come from Kuba. The other patterns are more or less closely allied to the neighbouring districts': Shirvan, Talish, Derbent, and the ornamentation of the Lesgh district, an inevitable consequence of the many exogamous marriages and tribal migrations down the centuries.

The 17th-century Armenian "dragon's head" rugs, too, are said to have been made at Kuba. But this is just unconfirmed guesswork.

Kuba rugs come in various qualities. None are sub-standard, and the best can be compared with Caucasians of very highest reputation. Very densely knotted, they have a short-shorn pile of strongly gleaming sheep's wool. Their basic tone is mostly dark indigo. If a people's temperament can be said to be reflected in its art, then Kuba is an excellent instance. The town had the same grim past as Derbent, the entire region being a corridor which all the conquerors of history passed through.

Kuba

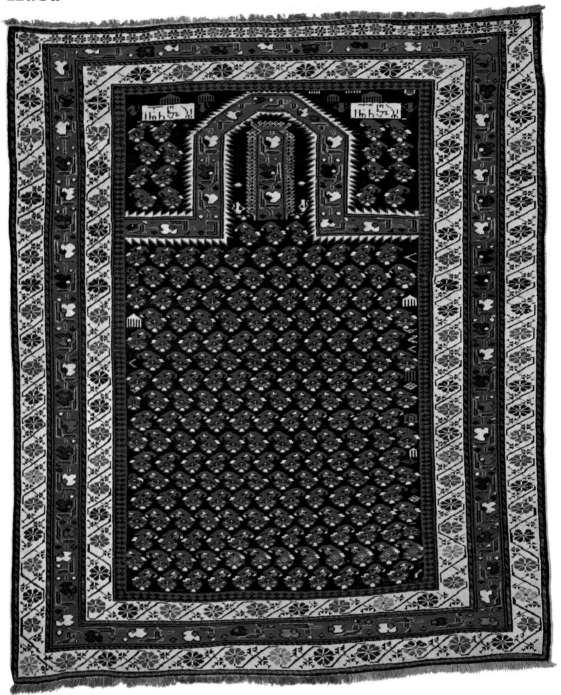

Significantly, even the prayer rugs have a dark ground tone. Another of the district's specialities is its carnation. These are also found on a Seichour carpet, the one with the "cabbage rose" design. Note the mirrored date on the prayer rug in the photo. It was copied by an illiterate rug-knotter from the back of some other rug, where the pattern was clearer.

The warp is mostly light, or light brown yarn.

Weft-threads are double and light.

The selvages are usually double, the outermost usually being light.

Belongs in the Daghestan group.

94

Kuba

Lambalo

PROTOTYPE of Lambalo rugs from Georgia.

The warp is light woollen thread. The fringes are usually artistically woven at the lower end.

Weft-threads are rusty red and usually three in number. Selvages are triple rust-red yarn. The rug is soft to the touch.

Worth noting: The Cross in the inner guard-band.

Belongs in the Kazak group.

Lenkoran

LENKORAN is on the Caspian Sea, in the southeast corner of Russian Azerbajdzjan. Its very name sounds grim to the Persians. Once it was a proud Persian fortress, with a garrison of some 4000 crack troops. The same year that Napoleon's army came to grief in the snows (1812), a Russian army marched across the snowy Moghan steppe and took Lenkoran by surprise. Its garrison was wiped out to the last man.

Lenkoran's status of garrison town explains why its output of rugs was not bigger; and thus their rarity. Worn they may have become; but certainly not threadbare. All exemplars still left in the trade are of very high quality.

Lenkoran is easily identified. The people who wove it seem to have had a Caucasian monopoly of the *tortoise figure*. In Persia it appears almost solely on the Malayer rug. Which of the two towns was the first to invent or use it, cannot today be determined. Lenkoran perhaps; because to Malayer's several dozen patterns, Lenkoran had only one. True, it could be varied: by slicing the tortoise in two, and combining the halves with the octagons of the neighbouring Moghans, or other geometrical motifs.

The ground tones are usually sombre, in rare cases ivory. No strong colours appear in the pattern. The warp, too, is dark, very often brownish; in the light carpets light undyed yarn. Weft-threads are brown or rusty brown. Single-thread selvages, as in Persian carpets; light on those with a light ground tone. Otherwise dark.

NB. To distinguish these from the Malayers, examine the back. The Malayer has a single weft-thread, thus exposing the warp at every other warp line! Lenkorans have *two* weft-threads which cover over and therefore conceal the warp.

Lesghi

THE LESGHIANS, with their 27 sub-tribes, are the biggest ethnic group in Daghestan. No one knows where they came from. Their language gives no clue.

One of the very first peoples to be converted by the Arabs to Islam in the 7th century, they acknowledged no ruler but the mullah, their religious leader. All Lesghian men were equals. A stumpy broad-shouldered race, for some unknown reason they still shave their heads. Formerly many had the four wives permitted by the Koran. If the husband died, his oldest son had to inherit all his women, willy-nilly. Excepting, of course, his own mother.

Born on horseback, with their dagger dangling from their umbilical chord, the Lesghians were a warrior, or rather robber, people. Attacking caravans and Georgian villages, they carried off all young men and women and children and sold them in the slave markets of Persia and Central Asia. It was a kind of hit-and-run tactics, but it left them time to vandalize churches, with their sabres striking off the heads of saints or, if painted on a wall, stabbing out their eyes.

The blood-feud was as sacred as hospitality. As long as a Lesghian had a guest in his house, he protected his life with his own. But it was perfectly in order to murder and rob him as soon as he'd left.

It was also the Lesghians who started the ruthless Jehad against the Russians, which they fought with such renowned fanaticism.

While the men made war, the women looked after the household and knotted rugs.

Their pattern, the "Lesghi Stars", is famous. True, their neighbours in the Shirvan district borrowed these stars to enhance their own pattern. But compete with the Lesghi it could not

The oblique stripes along the border are the Daghestan trade mark. Other elements are a hodge-podge of ornaments taken from various cultures: the falcon and other unidentifiable birds, King Solomon's stars, octagons, crabs, swastikas, S-s, and, among other things, a cruciform Assyrian quatrefoil, also found in the 2500 year-old Pazyryk Rug.

Qualitywise, Lesghis are among the very best. Even when new-made, their pile was short. Colours are as pellucid as Daghestan's high mountain air.

If the Lesghians prefer oblong rugs, it's because the stars show up better.

Warp, double weft-threads and selvages are all of light yearn.

Belongs in the Daghestan group.

Lori Pambak

PROTOTYPE of the Lori Pambak rug, from Georgia.

Warp: light yarn. Weft-threads two in number and brown. Selvages brown and mainly double. The rug feels very firm to the touch.

Worth noting: The little details differ as between its two halves. When about half the rug had been knotted, the work was taken over by someone else.

Belongs in the Kazak group.

Maresali

THIS IS a collector's item of the first water. In my view, Maresali made Caucasia's most attractive prayer-rugs.

Like other rugs from the Shirvan district, these are thin and finely knotted, the pile being cropped short from the beginning. Each tiny detail of ornament is as sharply visible to the eye as if it had been chiselled.

The field consists to 99% of the Mir-i-botah motif, each surrounded by a piece of zig-zag decoration reminiscent of a cockscomb. If a rug has some geometrical motif in its field, then the Mir-i-botahs will certainly appear in one of the guard bands, where they are reminiscent of chess knights.

Colour combinations can vary from veritable orgies of vivid hues to the most harmonious pastels. Border patterns vary widely, too.

Presumably larger rugs, too, were woven in Maresali; but have never appeared in the trade. It would be interesting to know why these nomads only sold their prayer-rugs and not the larger pieces — usually it's the other way round . . .

Most prayer-rugs measure about 145×100 cm.

The warp can as well be of light yarn as yarns of variegated colours, spun together. On the other hand, weft-threads and double selvages are always white.

Maresali

Mingrelian Rugs

HANDSOME is as handsome does. A saying applicable to the Mingrelian people and its rugs.

The Mingrelians are really Georgians. Up to the second half of the 15th century their country formed the western part of Georgia, but then it was divided up between various branches of their royal family. A most unsuitable moment for such a partition. The Ottomans had just captured Constantinople, and so had no difficulty in conquering the western half of the Caucasus.

The Georgians are a fine-looking people. Soon the Mingrelians saw their girls being carried off in tribute, to the Sultan's harem. If some potentate had peculiar tastes, the boys too. – Or else to the slave markets, chiefly for the same purpose.

Georgia has an ancient culture. Study of the Mingrelian rugs reveals them to be more sophisticated than the other Caucasians. Everything is tidy, elegant, symmetrical, tasteful. The rhomboid medallions in their field is the pattern most copied in Pakistani rugs. The Pakistanis regard Mingrelian as the prototype of all Caucasian rugs, calling their own "Kavkaz", after them.

The materials are admirable, and the colours discretly harmonious.

The warp is light, weft-threads double and whippings triple, almost black.

Belongs in the Kazak group.

Moghan

THESE RUGS get their name from the Moghan steppe, in the south-easternmost part of Russian Azerbaijan, where they were made.

What more can one say about a rug which only has one pattern? That it isn't original? For it isn't. Yet it's one of the most beautiful and authentic oriental patterns found anywhere between Turkmenistan and Turkey!

Or, again, I can point out how firm this rug is to the touch; tightly knotted and high-class. And so it is — but so what?

Or that its only fault is its extreme rarity. That too is a fact; and for good reasons. The steppe was thinly populated, and there was never any organized rug manufacture. How could there have been? Even to embark on a single rug was risky, and slim the chances of finishing it between two invasions or plundering raids. The steppe was a gateway, flung wide-open for all the hordes who arrived in the Caucasus by any route except the sea. Most came on horseback. Which was bad luck for the inhabitants of the Moghan steppe. And for us.

Warp and weft-threads are light, the double selvages brown.

Belongs in the Azerbaijan Group.

Ossetian Rugs

THE OSSETIANS – or Iranians, as they call themselves – live in the northern mountain districts of
Georgia. Ethnographers think they came in the
wake of Attila's Huns, from the banks of the
Don to Hungary. They are also supposed to
have given the Don and the Danube – Donau –
their names. In their tongue "don" means river.

Before the Russian Revolution they amounted
to some 300,000 souls, two-thirds Christian, the
rest Muslims. But there was not much difference
in their religious ideas: the Christians believed a
certain St. Elijah had saved mankind from a
dragon blind from birth. The Muslims thought
Mahomet had. But they saw eye to eye when it
came to stealing horses and plundering the
plain-dwellers.

They lived in round tower-like houses and had
no churchyards. Each family kept a similar
round house for its dead, thrusting the corpses in
through a little aperture. If a man died before his
wife, her right ear was cut off and flung in after
him, so he could claim her in the next world.

The dead were held in high respect. When
swearing an oath, a man had to hold a dog by its
tail; perjury, it was believed, was punished by the
perjuror's forebears having to eat up the dog.
So, no one swore a false oath: unthinkable for
the dead to have to chew a dog!

. The women's rugs were quite as bizarre. They
made them up on the "whatever comes to hand"
principle. Caring little if the colours had many
nuances where they should only have had one,
they were blissfully unaware of having created
something possessing what we like to call
"authentic nomad charm". Their blues shift like
the sky or the distant peaks of Kazbek, a blue
rare in the Kazak group.

Some of the ornaments seem abstract, among
them the one resemblange the letters H or K. The
former is fairly common in Afghan rugs. But
no one as yet knows its origin or meaning, if any.

The stepped motif in the main border, with the
rectangular hooks, is not found combined with
the usual "wineglass", as it is for instance in the
Chondoresk rug, but with a square on a stalk.
The border is optically confusing. The white
field can seem to be the actual motif. The
Russians, by the way, interpret the "wineglass"
as a "candlestick", and the "running dogs" in
the narrow guard-bands – a softer version of the
Greek meander pattern – as "twisted claws".

Warp light brown, likewise the fringes, if
surviving. Weft-threads, like the triple selvages,
are reddish brown.

Belongs in the Kazak group.

Perepedil

IF YOU'VE SEEN one of these, you've seen the lot. All appear to have been made on a single model. They are among the few overpatterned Caucasians.

The highly characteristic ornaments are:

1) The repeated rams' horns in the field.
2) Horizontal crosses along the inner guard-band. The shorter end of the cross is rounded like the handle of a clothe-hanger.
3) A mysterious animal you might take to be a swan or tortoise, if it didn't have six legs.

The rest of the field is stuffed with rhombs, octogons and various other motifs.

The rugs' quality is excellent, very densely knotted. The pile is short, and the wool has a high gleam.

Colours are predominantly dark, preferably with an indigo ground. Only a tiny minority have a light field.

Warp, the very thin weft-threads and the selvages are all of light undyed woollen yarn.

The rugs are made in the Kuba district.

Belongs in the Daghestan group.

Seichour

Good maps of the Caucasus have always been hard to come by. The ones from the 17th century show the Caspian Sea as a round puddle, not much bigger than a suburban swimming pool. Tribes are more commonly named than towns. A century later the maps began to take shape. Towns were now located, though their names, either misheard or hard to pronounce, were spelt wrong. Any traveller setting out with such a map must either be a brilliant linguist or an optimist, and have the sixth sense of a homing pigeon.

Even today Seichour is hard to find on a map. The Russians published no maps of the Caucasus and *those which do exist seem to have been drawn by hearsay — or anyway the ones which indicate the varieties of rugs.*

Seichour, at all events, lies south of Derbent, rather more than halfway to Kuba. Therefore Seichours are correctly placed in the Kuba district.

In the early 19th century, Seichour was still an insignificant little village. But 50 years later the rug export trade had got going, and Seichour had grown into an important small town.

A few years later, and a new pattern had been born. The Armenians had heard that their copatriates in Karabagh were doing a thriving trade supplying the "French Roses" design to the Russian market. And Seichour wanted its share of the cake. For lack of models it invented its own, taking the tea rose as model. The result looked more like a cabbage than a tea rose. For once in a while the trade found an appropriate name: "cabbage rose".

Today Seichours are rarities, much sought after. To the honour of the Seichour workshops let it be said they never lowered the quality, even though to have done so would have increased output and sold a lot more rugs.

The fibres are rich in animal fat, and it is this gives Seichours their fine shine. Colours, too, are fine; particularly the midnight blue of "cabbage rose" and the yellowish green of the ones bearing the "Georgian Cross".

The warp is of light yarn; likewise the very thin weft-threads.

Whipping is dark blue on "cabbage rose" and light on "Georgian Cross" examplars.

Belongs in the Daghestan group.

Sevan

WHEN ARMENIA'S borders were at their greatest extent, they comprised three great lakes: Van, Sevan, and Urmia. Now only Sevan is left. It was on its shore that one of Caucasia's most interesting carpets and the only 19th-century Armenian rug worth mentioning came into being: The Sevan.

Note particularly the overwhelming medallion, a gigantic Cross with butterfly wings. The trade also calls it "Butterfly Kazak" though only to clients, it sounds so much more romantic. However much respect and recognition the words imply, the rug itself needs neither adjectives nor romantic names.

The warp is of light undyed yarn. The two thin weft-threads are light brown. The double selvages, too, are of thin light brown yarn.

Belongs in the Kazak group.

Shirvan

SHIRVAN is a district in Daghestan. From here come the finest rugs in all Caucasia, at least for quality. Thin and densely knotted, their patterns are discreet and elegant. The colour combinations, often comprising light undyed yarn, are harmonious, sometimes in pastel shades throughout.

Rug-making was never organized in Shirvan.

Output could never keep up with demand, a factor which at all times has certainly helped to keep prices up.

Shirvan prayer-rugs, though rare, are in my view overvalued. Their aesthetic value does not correspond to the high prices you have to pay for them. Even the most beautiful design is inferior to the Maresali. Certain exemplars with grilles and honeycomb patterns on an off-white ground are often confused with the anonymous Daghestan prayer-rugs. Yet the Shirvan is a good deal narrower, about 80–90 cm., its prayer niche seeming squeezed from both sides.

The sizes of the other rugs range from about 100×60 cm. to 330×135 cm. — very rarely broader.

The standing of Shirvans is still so high that even the better Derbent and Kuba carpets are sometimes sold as Shirvans, presumably out of sheer ignorance. Neither a good Derbent nor a good Kuba needs to sail under false colours.

The rugs shown in the photos have been very carefully chosen. Their patterns are the ones most representative of the district. Even an amateur can easily identify the variants of Shirvan.

Usually the warp-threads consist of light and undyed brown sheepswool threads, spun together.

Weft-threads are light and very thin.

Selvages are without exception white over double or triple threads.

Belongs in the Daghestan group.

Shirvan

Soumaks

CAUCASIA has three types of woven rug. Soumak, Sile and Verneh. Note: woven, not knotted! The difference is that woven rugs have no pile, but a smooth flat surface.

The latter two not really being rugs and, very interesting though their patterns are, do not belong here. They are *kelims.* Fashionable in Europe in the early part of the century, people used them for curtains or bedcovers, as indeed the easterners did. Or else nailed them up on walls, which was more sensible than laying them on the floor.

Kelim fans, who use them as rugs – and many people do – probably won't share my opinion. Which is nevertheless well-grounded. Again and again I've almost broken my neck on some kelim laid without a rubber underlay on plastic-treated parquet flooring.

But the Soumak is different. The pattern on a Sile or a Verneh is visible on both sides. On a Soumak, only from the front! Threads of yarn, four to six centimetres long, have been left hanging on the back. This makes it heavier; so you can walk on it without any rubber underlay – providing you're properly insured and have two guardian angels.

Personally, I've always favoured rubber underlay for *any* rug, both for its sake and my own. In the Caucasus, where there's little danger of slipping up on any floor, they lay a stamped felt under the Soumak.

As a textile it is admirable. The saddlecloth on p. 130 measures only some 155 × 110 cm. Study of the pattern's many little details reveals how much art and craftsmanship has gone into it.

The picture on p. 131 shows the prototype. All Soumak rugs look like this, the differences being insignificant. Those with an indigo ground tone are thought to be older than the red ones. At all events they are rarer. And more expensive.

Sizes vary from little squares, used for cushion covers or the faces of storage bags, up to about 350 × 250 cm.

If you like the Soumak, that's fine. If you happen to have one at home, don't forget the underlay!

Belongs in the Daghestan group.

Svanian

THE SVANIANS are one of Georgia's many bizarre mountain tribes. Allergic to taxes, regulations and bullying officials, rather than submit to being civilized they preferred to flee up into the high mountain valleys.

Officially Christian, their religious ideas were off-beat. Heaven was an immense grazing ground, and hell a sea of boiling tar. They sacrificed lambs to the gods of hunting and plunder – their two most important deities. Hunting and plundering lowland villages were their favourite pastimes.

The sons were brought up at an early age to hunt and make war. Eight-year old boys rode and handled firearms. Oddly, they still suckled, if not their mothers, then going from breast to breast amidst wet-nurses like bees among flowers. The milk of these high altitude Caucasian women must have had something about it – its packaging apart – if eight-year-olds could participate in the grown ups' hunting and pillaging expeditions!

The women's hobbies were less exciting. They looked after the home and the animals, and then, in their "spare time", sat down at their looms.

The rugs they knotted were poor quality. But the pattern was more interesting. The outer "harlequin" border is careless. The S-border is squeezed into nonentity. An extra border on the upper end shows a disarmingly naive and asymmetrical collection of stars, birds and half-finished flights of fancy. Only the rectangular hooks around the medallions are properly finished off; and these suggest a Central Asian origin. The most amusing detail is the two human figures down in the righthand corner. The white one has come from heaven – or else is on his way thither – whilst the dark one has come straight out of the bath of tar. His white hands? Well, maybe he was innocent after all . . .

Yarn and colours give no cause for complaint; only the quality. These carpets are loosely knotted, and most were soon worn out. Yet many collectors like them; regard them as having the "unsophisticated charm of the nomad".

The warp is light, grey or of mingled yarn.

Weft-threads are double and in their natural colour – grey.

The selvage is double and brown.

Belongs in the Kazak group.

Talish

THE TALISH district lies in the South-eastern Caucasus.

Although Talish borders on Persian Azerbaijan – and, indeed, for long periods, was a Persian province nothing could prevail on its rug-makers to ape Persian patterns.

If there was any influence, it came from Samarkand. The rug on the opposite page has the *correct border,* decorated with Mongolian ornaments.

The left-hand rug on p. 136 has both Chinese and Daghestan décor; its carnations come from the Kuba district. But the one on the right is a "bastard" carpet; can only have been a product of exogamy. The honeycomb pattern is from the Shirvan district in Daghestan. Neither is the border genuine Talish.

For some mysterious reason most rugs made in Germi, Udshali, Drich and the other ancient villages were corridor rugs, *the one with the correct border and a monochrome unpatterned field, the so-called "Met-hane" design, being the most valuable.*

In my view, though, despite their good quality and the beauty of the "Met-hane" pattern – particularly if the field is indigo or sky-blue – they are over-valued. But, as I've said elsewhere, the price is what people will pay at auction.

The warp, weft-threads and selvages are all in light yarn.

Lenkoran and Moghan are also regarded as belonging in the Talish district, though all three fall in the Azerbaijan group.

Talish

Index

*Numbers in italic refer to pages
where illustrations may be found*

Both author and publisher wish to express their gratitude to Mr. Alexander Juran, London, for allowing some forty of his superb collection of his rugs to be photographed.

Also to Mme M. Schapira, London, for lending us five rugs out of her collection, for the same purpose. All the others shown in this book belong or have belonged to the author.

My admiration and thanks to all those students and travellers who, having criss-crossed that remarkable part of the globe known as the Caucasus, have passed on their knowledge and experience of its crumbling ancient human mosaics. Few though they are, alas, such persons are too numerous, even so, for individual mention.

N.F.